Finding Love

A Paperback Original
First published 1989 by
Poolbeg Press Ltd.
Knocksedan House,
Swords, Co. Dublin, Ireland.

ISBN 1 85371 026 1

Cover design by Steven Hope
Typeset by Print-Forme,
62 Santry Close, Dublin 9.
Printed by The Guernsey Press Ltd.,
Vale, Guernsey, Channel Islands.

Finding Love
Gabriel Kiely

POOLBEG

To
Linda

Preface

Dear Reader

This is a book for people in long-term relationships. In writing it, I think of many couples who struggled for a better relationship. Their pain, their hopes, and their resolve to address profound and intimate problems was its inspiration. While the book has grown from my work as a marital therapist, its message applies equally to any couple who want to enhance their own relationship. The search of every married couple for explanations and insights is one of the main concerns of this book. Its message is universal and is one of hope.

Marriage is both a personal experience and a social institution. How we live out our intimate relationships is affected by what happens in society as well as by what we bring to them as individuals. As society changes, so too do marriages and these changes are not just at an institutional level, but also at a personal level. This is the main premise underlying the approach to marital therapy in this book.

The current theoretical base and clinical practice in marital therapy do not take sufficient account of the findings of many social scientists on the evolution of marriage in modern Western society. Failure to take account of these findings is particularly evident in the case of some couples who experience marital unhappiness because of their changed expectations of marriage. Awareness of the effects that social change may have had on these changing expectations may help some couples to re-invest in their relationships.

Reinvestment Therapy is an original approach for working with couples experiencing marital difficulties. The approach was developed during a study conducted in a Dublin Community Psychiatric Clinic. The argument underlying the approach is based on the notion of marriage as a specialised institution for meeting people's needs for affection. This institution has been going through a period of rapid change which is characterized by the development of companionship marriage where negotiated roles and the meeting of people's needs for affection have increasingly become the core of the relationship.

Reinvestment Therapy firstly tackles the feelings of guilt and failure that derive from an unhappy relationship. Too often these feelings are re-inforced by therapeutic approaches that treat such relationships as being somehow pathological. Reinvestment Therapy does not assume that couples automatically commit themselves to continuing the relationship simply by requesting counselling. Re-investment is a choice the individual must make to renegotiate the relationship on the basis of a new commitment.

In addition to Reinvestment Therapy, the book presents many practical guides for the marital therapist. Much of this material was revealed by a content analysis of the case records of the couples in the study. It includes indicators of marital therapy that reflect a couple's movement towards a resolution of their relationship problems and therapy goals that are applicable to any couple. A short-term treatment model for use in marital therpy is also examined and explained. Finally, some of the implications of the material contained in this book are discussed in terms of the challenges they present to couples, marital therapists and society in general.

The setting of the original study was important in pointing to the conclusion that unhappiness in relationships can be related to social change, and does not necessarily imply personal inadequacy. The setting was significant because it was a psychiatric clinic. Many of the couples seen for marital therapy were likely to have had one or both partners initially showing some sort of psychiatric symptom. This is an important factor because one might conclude that couples presenting with psychiatric symptoms (with labels such as depression) might well find the cause of their unhappiness in some underlying psychiatric problem. On the contrary, for many of the couples in this study, this was not the case. Their "symptoms" were frequently stress reactions to an unhappy relationship.

The study was made possible by the help of many people along the way. Among them is the late Dr Desmond McCarthy, Clinical Director of Cluain Mhuire Family Centre, whose encouragement during the time of the study was immensely helpful. I am indebted to Brother Jarleth Crilly, former Secretary/ Manager of the centre, for his co-operation and friendship. Additional thanks go to the Eastern Health Board who supported the project by their grant to the

Department of Social Science, University College Dublin. Thanks are likewise due to University College Dublin itself for its grant-aid towards the cost of publication of this book. My gratitude goes also to Terese Tomich and the staff of Catholic Social Services of Los Angeles all of whom played a major part in my development as a social worker.

I wish to express my appreciation of my colleagues in the Family Studies Centre, Department of Social Science, University College Dublin, especially Dr Helen Burke and Dr Patrick Clancy, for their invaluable help with various parts of the original study, and to Imelda McCarthy, for her many useful comments on the final draft. Thanks also to Catherine Rose for her editorial support and encouragement and to both Dan O'Shea and Dominic Murdock of St Patrick's College, Maynooth for their computer assistance. A special thanks to Jo O'Donoghue of Poolbeg Press for her help in bringing this book to publication. Finally, my warmest thanks to Linda Kiely for her suggestions, insights, constant encouragement, patience, confidence, work and above all her love all through the writing of this book, and to our four children who endured its writing.

Contents

Chapter   page

1   Marriage in Crisis: a Personal Failure?   1

2   The Search for Love   12

3   Changing Relationships in Changing Times   18

4   Compatibility in Marriage   38

5   Specialization in Marriage   49

6   Reinvestment Therapy Explained   56

7   Measuring Success   76

8   Goal Setting   93

9   Reinvestment Therapy—a Short-Term Treatment   119

10   The Challenge of Reinvestment Therapy   130

      Bibliography   143

Chapter 1

Marriage in Crisis: a Personal Failure?

Why do some people's relationships end while others succeed? Obviously there is no easy answer. Neither is there only one answer. People's marriages can be unhappy for a variety of reasons. But can it be said as a general statement, that if a person's relationship is not successful, then the most likely place to find the reasons for this is in the personality or individual make-up of one or both partners in the relationship? In other words, is marital unhappiness a personal failure?

Let us take the case of Jimmy and Eileen. When their relationship was breaking down, they repeatedly asked each other, "Why can't we get along together when we have everything going for us: a good home, nice children, secure employment, caring friends and relatives?" To find the answer they came back again and again to a questioning of their own personal adequacy. "Am I dependent, immature, selfish, sick, impatient, neurotic?" "Is my husband sick?" "Is my wife going through the change of life?" All the questions had one thing in common: they were all ways of asking, "What is wrong with me, you or both of us?"

This type of question reflects an attitude about

1

marriage that seems to prevail in modern Western society. This attitude in effect appears to assume that if you are unable to make a success of your marriage, then someone in that marriage must be immature, emotionally unstable, or possibly even suffering from some hidden mental disorder that is not readily visible to the ordinary person. As a result, many people experiencing unhappiness in their relationship are confronted not only with the stress arising out of their unhappiness, but also with feelings of failure because of society's attitude towards them.

This attitude is found in many places, the literature on marital therapy itself being one. For example, Jack Dominian, a well-known authority on marital breakdown, states that "the vast majority of marriages which run into serious conflict do so in the presence of marked personality disturbance."[1] The same theme is reflected in the writings of Bannister and Pincus from the Marital Unit of the Tavistock Clinic.[2] Also, Dr. Skynner in his book *One Flesh: Separate Persons* takes a similar attitude to problems of individuals in marriage.[3] Much the same trend runs through the papers in Dryden's book, *Marital Therapy in Britain*.[4] The suggestion here is not that these experts necessarily claim that every marital problem is a result of personal inadequacy. The point, however, is that in their writings they seem to place an emphasis on personality factors, and it is this emphasis that is significant.

This attitude is also reflected in other aspects of society, for example in legal systems which "require one spouse to charge the other with marital misconduct in order to obtain a divorce."[5] The underlying premise here is that if the marriage has come to the point when it is no longer a viable relationship, then it must be somebody's fault. This surely reflects the view that marital breakdown is directly attributable to the failure of one or other of the partners. While it must be said that a change in this attitude is reflected in the introduction of no-fault divorce in a many countries, the retention of adversarial approaches in marital breakdown testifies to its prevalence. There are many places where the adversary system is still in operation.

The notion that marital unhappiness is a result of personal inadequacy seems to prevail even when high percentages of marriages end in divorce. If this attitude reflects reality, then there are a lot of unstable, immature, and emotionally unhealthy people around. In fact, in some cases the numbers are so high that it should lead to our questioning the whole notion of normality, at least as it applies to marriage.

Let us return to Eileen and Jimmy. When they came for marital therapy neither of them could be seen as immature or emotionally unstable. They had been married for twelve years and had two children aged ten and eight. Since the second child started school, Eileen had been working full-time as a teacher. Jimmy was in middle management and found his job stimulating and challenging. They owned their own home and liked where they were living. They got along well with relatives and seemed to have good relationships at work. They went on family holidays, participated in community events and considered themselves active members of their Church. Jimmy and Eileen were both outgoing, friendly people who appeared to have everything going for them. Why, then, did their marriage seem to be in danger of breakdown?

Any attempt to understand their marital problem in terms of personality proved to be inadequate. It was necessary to look elsewhere for an explanation. Underlying their marital difficulties was the fact that neither felt understood by the other. For example, when Eileen felt under pressure at work she would become unresponsive to Jimmy's need for emotional closeness and busy herself with classroom preparation. Jimmy saw this as withdrawal from him and felt alone and even rejected. His attempts to explain this to Eileen usually led to an argument which resulted in both of them feeling isolated and misunderstood. This feeling of being misunderstood was creating a major rift between them, to the point where Jimmy felt he no longer loved Eileen. This in turn affected their sexual life which then became one part in a whole chain of inter-related cause and effect consequences. It could be said that Eileen's solution to the problem of Jimmy's need for closeness, i.e. her busying herself with classroom preparation, had now become a problem for Jimmy.

Likewise, it is easy to see why they focused on their sexual problem when they first came for marital therapy. By focusing on this "problem" they allowed themselves to believe that the cause of their marital unhappiness lay in some personal or sexual inadequacy. This, in a sense, provided a "solution" for the other more fundamental aspects of their interaction.

Jimmy and Eileen were relatively easy to help once

they began to see that their sexual problem was a reflection of their emotional distance from each other, and might even be providing an excuse in the guise of a "solution" for not dealing with their more basic difficulty. Motivated by their strong desire to stay together, they willingly used the techniques suggested and successfully closed this distance.

Janice and Paul are another couple whose marital difficulties could not be adequately understood by means of the more traditional explanations of marital breakdown. Paul, a plumber, had worked for the same company since before he was married. He liked his work and was financially secure. He and Janice had four children, all of school-going age except for the youngest who was three years old. Janice looked after other children in her home as an additional source of income. She liked the little financial independence it gave her. Paul and Janice, like Jimmy and Eileen, were both outgoing and led full lives. But, they, too, were on the brink of marital breakdowm when they sought therapy.

One of the underlying problems with Paul and Janice was that they had different ideas about marriage. While Paul did not object to Janice making some additional money for herself, he felt that his contribution to their marriage was to provide a "decent standard of living." In turn, Janice should perform the basic tasks of housekeeping. Paul assisted her with some of these tasks, but essentially felt that in doing so, he was doing her a favour. In the evenings he watched television or sometimes fell asleep on the couch if his day at work had been particularly demanding. As far as Paul was concerned, he was the perfect husband, especially when he compared himself to his friends.

Janice, on the other hand, had different ideas about their marriage She felt that Paul provided her with little if any companionship; that he did not listen to her and took for granted her love and loyalty. She also felt that Paul seldom gave her emotional support except in times of crisis (such as the death of a close relative), and then Janice felt he did so in a manner that made her feel that she was weak and that he was strong.

Janice and Paul were indeed in trouble. Trying to explain their different views about marriage using a personal inadequacy model was not going to be much help in finding a solution for them. When they realized that their having different views about marriage was one of the main factors underlying their conflicts, they were less angry and less defensive, as this realization in turn lifted the burden of personal fault that was further polarizing them. They each developed the ability to listen to what the other was saying without interrupting and were eventually able to move towards a relationship that included some of the essential aspects of their respective expectations.

Both of these cases are typical of the marital unhappiness experienced by many couples in today's society. Each of them reflects aspects of societal change, and the effect of this change on marriage. Jimmy and Eileen were affected by the increased emphasis on personal fulfilment in modern Western society. With the struggle for material survival appearing to be at an end in the modern Western world, people's attention has increasingly become focused on the quality of life.

It is worth noting, however, that while the focus of

modern society might well be on the "quality of life," there are many people who are still contending with severe material deprivation. For them the struggle for material survival is far from being at an end. For many the achievement of material prosperity is more an illustion than a reality. It is an illusion created in large part by the promises of advertising and the unreal expectations encouraged by the "welfare state." Whether the end of the struggle for Jimmy and Eileen was an illusion or a reality, they, like many others, were increasingly focusing on the quality of life.

This change in focus has meant that in addition to anticipating material well-being, people have increased expectations of personal fulfilment which in the context of marriage mean far greater expectations of emotional support and understanding. For Jimmy and Eileen this focus was reflected in their search for fulfilment in their relationship with each other. Had they not had these expectations, it is likely that they would have had a "happy" marriage. The origins of their unhappiness could be said to lie in change in society and consequent changes in attitudes.

The problems of Paul and Janice reflect other changes in society. These include changed attitudes towards women, and changed expectations of marriage. Paul continued to relate to Janice as if none of these changes had taken place. Janice saw marriage as providing companionship and she saw her place in the relationship of marriage as equal to that of her husband.

The vast literature and extensive research findings in the broad area of social theory are left largely unapplied when it comes to understanding the marriages of individual couples. While some books and manuals on marriage refer to aspects of this literature, there is little evidence of its use in actual practice.[6] The more one applies some of this material to understanding individual marital problems, the clearer it becomes that many couples experience marital unhappiness for reasons other than those that have their origin in personality problems.

Couples experiencing marital dissatisfaction do not form a homogeneous group to which one explanation alone can be applied. Some couples experience marital dissatisfaction because of personality disturbance, some for other reasons. It follows then that approaches to marital therapy must relate to the various causes of marital dissatisfaction.

A basic assumption of Reinvestment Therapy, the approach used in this book, is that some couples experience marital dissatisfaction as a result of social change and the effects of that change on modern marriage. Up to now, these couples have not been identified as a separate category in the field of marital therapy requiring, as they do, an approach different to those that rely heavily on personality theory. To view a couple's inability to meet each other's affectional needs (i.e. the need for love and affection) solely in the context of their individual personalities and/or negative childhood experiences, is to ignore the effects of social change on marriage. Marriages are not free standing, independent social units unaffected by social change. Just as the institution of marriage is changing in response to changes in society, so too are individual marriages. Couples experiencing marital unhappiness because of these changes must be seen within this context. If marital therapists are to respond in a meaningful and helpful way to these couples when they request help, then the approach to marital therapy they use should be based on the reasons for the particular couple's unhappiness.

So, to answer the question, "Is marital unhappiness always the result of personal failure?" the answer for many couples must be "No." It is true, however, that the unhappiness may be experienced or felt as a personal failure. To say, however, that all unhappiness in marriage is a personal failure is to judge individuals as being responsible for the forces of social change. Just as material poverty cannot be understood simply by understanding the individuals who are poor, neither can marital unhappiness be understood solely by understanding the personalities of those who are unhappy in marriage.

This book is concerned with the impact of social change on marriage. It is not an attempt to replace any one explanation for marital unhappiness with another. Marriages are personal relationships. Thus, we need to draw from a wide range of theory, including both psychological and sociological theory, in order to understand fully the dynamics of individual marriages. In the field of marital therapy the focus has traditionally been on the psychological explanations for marital unhappiness and as such has tended to look to the personalities of the individuals who are married. By highlighting the social theory dimensions of marriage, this book suggests that for some couples at least, an explanation for marital unhappiness may be more appropriately located in the social context of their relationship. Essentially this means that changes in society have brought about changes in marriage. These changes are reflected in an increase in expectations that marriage will meet the affectional needs of the partners. For many couples fulfilling these expectations requires a reinvestment in their marriage in order to find and expand sources of affection. This reinvestment is what much of this book is about.

Reinvestment Therapy, however, is not suitable for use with all couples experiencing marital difficulties. For example, when one partner in the marriage is addicted to alcohol, there is little use in trying to secure a commitment to changing interaction with his/her spouse when much of the person's behaviour is controlled by the addiction. The addiction would have to be addressed first, as the approach to marital therapy discussed here assumes that both partners want change and are capable of changing their relationship. Likewise, the existence of any major personality problem would counter-indicate the use of Reinvestment Therapy. However, much of what is contained in this book applies to all marriage. Couples in alcoholic marriages, who experience the pain of unfulfilled expectations just like couples in any other marriage, can also experience the joy of their fulfilment.

NOTES

1. J. Dominian, *Marital Breakdown* (Harmondsworth 1968), p. 105

2. K. Bannister and L. Pinus, *Shared Phantasy in Marital Problems: Therapy in a Four-Person Relationship* (London 1976)

3. A. Skynner, *One Flesh: Separate Persons* (London 1976)

4. W. Dryden, ed., *Marital Therapy in Britain* (London 1985)

5. S. Bahr, "Marital Dissolution Laws", *Journal of Family Issues* September 1983, pp.455-66.

6. Many approaches in Family Therapy do not rely on personal factors. See for example H. R. Maturana and F. J. Varela *The Tree of Knowledge: The Biological Roots of Human Understanding* (Boston 1987); B. Carter and M. McGoldrick *The Changing Family Life Cycle* (New York 1988) and H. Anderson and H. A. Goolishan "Human Systems as Linguistic Systems: Preliminary and Evolving Ideas about the Implications for Clinical Theory." *Family Process* 27. 1988. pp.371-393.

Chapter 2

The Search for Love

A reason frequently given by couples for their marital problems is that they feel they no longer love each other. This complaint comes in many forms. For example, it might be expressed by depression, excessive drinking, an extra-marital affair or violence. While these symptoms do not always reflect a lack of love, the lack of love in marriage is frequently expressed in these ways. Depression can be the feeling of loneliness and isolation resulting from unfulfilled expectations of love. Excessive drinking can be an escape. Extra-marital affairs are often the result of feeling unloved. Violence in marriage, be it verbal or physical, is frequently an attack on the person who is seen to be witholding love.

Some couples who are in severe marital conflict might well claim to love each other. This claim is made even when their experience of each other is almost exclusively destructive. Yet, in spite of the pain they feel inflicted on them by their relationship, they seem unable to acknowledge that they do not love one another. Such an admission can be seen by them as the death-knell of their marriage, so they cling to the illusion more as a denial of the severity of their conflict than a confirmation of their investment in each other.

Love has many forms. There is the love of a child for a parent, the love of an exile for the homeland, the love of a friend for a friend, love for mankind in general and love of God. And there is love in marriage. The nature of love is extensively treated in many fields, especially by philosophy. Yet, as Toner points out, whatever its nature, most people think of love as: " ... that mysterious element in unanalysed human experience which is the deepest moving force of human activity. The literature of all times and cultures testifies to this natural conviction."[1]

Love is defined in Cassell's *English Dictionary* as a "feeling of deep regard, fondness and devotion." It is an emotional rather than an intellectual process and its primary expression in human experience is found in the relationship between children and parents. It is also found in relationships between adults. Reiss describes the development of love as consisting of a movement from a feeling of rapport to self-revelation, and the development of mutual dependencies and finally to personality need fulfilment.[2]

As used here, love can have several forms or varieties, of which romantic love is but one. As with love, many definitions of romantic love can be found. Shorter defines it as "the capacity for spontaneity and empathy in an erotic relationship"[3] Dominian describes it as "an engrossing emotional attachment between a man and a woman exclusive and individualized, transcending at need all sorts of obstacles involving some kind of idolization, and enveloping the sex relationship in an aura of tender sentiment for the personality of the loved ones."[4]

Burgess and Locke identify six processes essential

for romantic love. Four of them are almost identical to those listed by Reiss above in his description of love. The other two are idolization and sexual behaviour.[5]

It seems, then, that sexual attraction and some idolization of the loved person are the features that make love "romantic."

The term affection rather than romantic love is used in this work as it more accurately denotes the function fulfilled by modern marriage in Western society. Affection may include love, but the absence of love does not negate the existence of affection. The two can be synonomous depending on the definitions used. In fact, it is possible to distinguish between affection, love, and romantic love. However, both affection and romantic love are essentially variations on the theme of love.

In marital therapy, couples often struggle over the question of whether or not they love each other. To answer "no" can be seen as a rejection of the other person. To answer "yes" might belie the loneliness felt in an unfulfilling relationship. And then there is the difference between feeling that you love someone and the feeling of being loved in return. The irony in all of this is that the answer itself is of little consequence. What does it matter how you answer the question if you consistently act in an unloving way?

Since the answer to the question is not important, then what is the significance of love in contemporary marriage? The distinction here is between how a couple answer a particular question, and the nature and function of love in *that* relationship. Undoubtedly, love plays a central role in many marriages. For some , love may be the primary bond in the relationship, its function clearly being the uniting element. For others, love is seen as an added bonus, but not central to the continuance of the relationship. For these couples, marriage is seen to have other functions valued by them as of greater significance.

The case of Rose and Larry illustrates a struggle over whether love existed or not. Larry said that he could not act in a caring, affectionate way towards Rose because he felt that he no longer loved her. Yet, he came for marital therapy, and was sincere in his desire to build a new relationship with Rose. For him, his focus on the presence or absence of "feelings" of love were blocking him from making any changes in the marriage. To act lovingly, which indispensably means caringly, meant for him that he would not be true to his feelings. It was not until he was able to see that the hurt generated by their patterns of interaction precluded feelings of love, that he was able to begin to change. The new patterns they constructed resulted in a changed emotional climate which in turn permitted the affection that Larry originally complained of not having when he felt he no longer loved Rose.

The term "affection" is used because it describes the satisfaction of the basic human need for emotional understanding and support. As such, it is related to the need for acceptance and approval as manifested in the feeling of being appreciated for oneself. The feelings of emotional bliss that are customarily associated with romantic love are not a necessary component of affection, but often accompany it. An affectional relationship is one where each person feels cared for as a person by the other.

Winch's need-based theory of love provides a good

framework for understanding the use of the term affection. He describes love as the positive emotion experienced in an interpersonal relationship when an individual's social needs are met. To differentiate them from physical needs, he identified social needs as mental or emotional dissatisfactions. The need to love and to be loved is experienced as a result of socialization, the same as the need for acceptance and security.[6] Much of this theory is based on Freudian concepts of separation anxiety. This anxiety has its origin in the parent-child relationship. Its central feature is that separation results in a sense of loneliness, consisting of a feeling of not belonging or of not being accepted. According to this reasoning, theoretically at least, people should have a feeling of being loved when they feel a sense of belonging and of being accepted. This is the way the term affection is being used here. Winch, in fact, acknowledges that his definition of love can also apply to affection, the difference being mainly one of intensity.[7]

The emphasis on the meeting of affectional needs in marriage, rather than on the exchange of love, is deliberate. Couples experiencing severe relationship difficulties are unlikely to be meeting each other's social needs, as identified above. They are unlikely to "feel" love for each other whether or not they are willing to acknowledge this. It seems, therefore, to be less confusing to talk about meeting affectional needs both in the general theoretical discussions of marital happiness and directly with individual couples who are experiencing marital unhappiness rather than to focus on the presence or absence of "love."

Couples certainly expect to find love in marriage. It

is highly unusual if not impossible to find a couple who feel needed, accepted and approved of by each other but who are not in love. A couple who come seeking marital therapy for the sake of "the children" or because of their belief in the indissolubility of marriage, are not likely to find love unless they can at least add to these reasons, if not replace them with a desire to have a full and complete relationship with each other. This desire needs to be unconditional and unique to the people involved. It is only with such an approach that they are likely to develop mutual affection and find the moonlight and roses that sadly are all too often abandoned as an unattainable illusion.

NOTES

1. J. Toner, *The Experience of Love* (Washington 1968), p. 17.

2. I. Reiss,"Towards a Sociology of the Heterosexual Love Relationship," *Marriage and Family Living* (May 1960), pp. 139-45.

3. E. Shorter, *The Making of the Modern Family* (London 1976), p. 15

4. J. Dominian, *op.cit.*, p. 11.

5. E. Burgess, H. Locke and M. Thomes, *The Family: From Institution to Companionship* 4th ed. (New York, 1971), p.68.

6. R. Winch,*The Modern Family* , rev. ed. (New York, 1963), pp. 569-81.

7. *Ibid*, p. 580

Chapter 3

Changing Relationships in Changing Times

Barbara is twenty-seven years old and lives alone with her two children. Her marriage to Ken ended one year ago when she found out that he was involved with another woman. At first they both sought marital therapy. They presented as mature adults. Neither showed any signs of emotional or psychological problems apart from the normal reactions to their marital stress. After a few sessions, Barbara discontinued coming for therapy because Ken would not agree to breaking off his relationship with the other woman, Helen. Ken and Helen now live together while Barbara is trying to start a new life for herself.

The situation of Ken and Barbara is typical of what is happening to many couples whose marriages end in separation. That is, they are confronted with one or more problems in their relationship which they are unable to resolve. They then focus their attention and energies on these problems instead of on underlying conditions which might have brought them about in the first place. Because of this they are unable to find satisfactory solutions. Their level of frustration and anger increases and finally, almost in desperation, one or other of them feels that he/she can no longer continue to live in such a relationship. The stated reason why the relationship ends may vary. For some couples, the relationship ends because one of the partners, like Ken, has become involved in a new relationship. Other reasons often include interference by in-laws, inability to communicate, lack of emotional support and myriad other complaints that have become all too familiar in recent years.

On closer examination, however, many of these complaints seem to have one major feature in common. That is, either one or both of the partners are saying "I no longer feel that I love you." Apart from mental and emotional disorders this absence of positive emotional exchange is probably the most significant factor that leads to unhappiness.

Why does affection play such a significant role in today's marriages? To find the answer, we have to see marriage in the context of the many changes that have occurred in society over the last few decades, and the effects of these changes on marriage and the family.[1] In response to what is happening in society, marriage is going through a process of change and this change is manifested primarily in the nature of the emotional bond that unites couples in modern marriage. The change is often characterised by a transition from what is thought of as the "traditional" family to the "modern" family. These two types of family, or more correctly, ways of thinking about the family, can also be called "institutional" and "companionship" families.[2] These latter names emphasize chacteristics of the family types, such as the institutional or the companionship nature of the family, rather than the period when they occurred in history, as might be suggested by referring to them as traditional or modern families.

We find then, two types of families. Neither type is necessarily better or worse than the other. They are simply different. The institutional type refers to families where relationships are based on specified duties and traditional roles. For example, each partner in the marriage is likely to have clearly defined jobs that are determined by the person's sex. The companionship family type is unlikely to reflect duty as a major bond in its relationships. It is characterised by bonds based on love and affection.

The difference between these two types, institutional and companionship, is a matter of emphasis. Institutional marriage may also value love, and companionship marriage, duty. If Ken and Barbara had an institutional orientation to their marriage, it is possible that duty, being a primary bond in an institutional marriage, would have out-weighed their disillusionment with love and that it would therefore have maintained their marriage, at least as legally constituted.

In a way Barbara and Ken reflect changes in society. Their need for greater closeness is linked to an increased emphasis on companionship in marriage. None of these societal changes on their own can be described as having brought about the changes in marriage, but when they are interconnected with others, the conclusion seems almost inescapable. For example, the connection between the increased employment of married women outside the home—something brought about by changing economic conditions—and the freedom for women resulting from the contraception revolution illustrate this. The first makes possible the freedom of women on a macro-level while the exercise of this freedom remains largely dependent on the micro-level freedom permitted by the use of effective means of contraception. Together these changes have had a profound effect on marriage.

Among the changes occurring in society that have affected marriage and the family are: changed family functions and roles; increased economic freedom for women; the movement towards gender equality and changed attitudes towards sex. These changes are identified not because they represent all changes, but because they clearly show the impact of change in the larger social system, i.e. society, on the individual relationships of those in the smaller social system, i.e. marriage.

Let us first look at changes in family functions. The family as a basic social unit in Western society performs specific functions or tasks, both for society and for its individual members. Any social system, such as a school, a bank or a factory, has a function. The school teaches; the bank exchanges money; the factory produces a product. Most systems have more than one function. For example, the school socializes the young as well as teaching them. Likewise the family has more than one function.

In the work of writers on the family there can be found various listings of these functions. Ogburn, for example, enumerates the functions traditional to the family as educational, economic, affectional, religious, protective, recreational, prestigious and status-giving.[3] Parsons lists them as the "socialization of the child, and the stabilization of the adult personalities of the population of the society."[4] Coser, in concluding her review on the functions of the family, while claiming not to provide a list herself, identifies the main functions of the family as the institutionalization of social fatherhood; the establishment through marriage of alliances outside of blood relations; the imposition of social norms on the biological organisms; and the bestowing of social identity on its members.[5] From among the various listings it can be seen that the family serves to meet individuals' needs for affection and also to meet the social needs of the parents. On behalf of society, the family provides for the achievement of reproduction and socialization. It should be noted, however, that the family does not have a monopoly on any of these functions and that the number of functions may vary from family to family.

Apart from this sharing of functions and individual variations, the family as a social system has transferred to other social systems, either in whole or in part, some functions that it traditionally fulfilled. For example, most of the protective functions are now performed almost exclusively by the state through the police; and at least a minimum of food and shelter is provided through social welfare services. Education is also provided outside of the family with parents increasingly transferring their role as educators to schools. The same is true for the economic and recreational functions. Even some responsibility for parenting has been transferred to the state with the state's acceptance not only of the provision of substitute parenting, but also in its acceptance of ultimate parental responsibility for the care of all children.[6]

These changes in the family represented by the lessening of its functions do not necessarily indicate a breakdown of the family as a social institution. As Parsons suggests, they more accurately reflect a process of re-organization rather than the disintegration of the family.[7] Basically, this re-organization means that the family with fewer functions to perform is becoming a more specialized social system. In the case of marriage, which is a sub-system within the family, this increased specialization has meant a greater emphasis on the emotional importance of the "significant person" of the opposite sex.[8]

In other words, companionship, one of the traditional functions of marriage, is becoming increasingly important within marriage as other functions are transferred to other social systems. However, like any other system, such as an industry that produces only one product, the fewer the functions, the greater the specialization, and the greater the risk of collapse if the specialized product runs into difficulty.

A second area of change has to do with the economic position of women. One well-documented result of industrialization, especially in the 20th century, has been increased prosperity. One only has to look at the increase in the gross national product of most Western countries to verify this fact. This prosperity has brought an economic freedom to family members that was non-existent in pre-industrial society, where physical survival depended on membership of a close working group, such as the family, which produced the goods it consumed. At that time, to move out of the family group was tantamount in most cases to selecting abject poverty or indeed death by starvation and exposure. This is no longer the case in the Western world. With the fight for survival mastered, attention is directed to the quality of survival. Even if this mastery is doubtful, people seem be governed by the illusion that survival itself no longer requires a major struggle.

The economic freedom of women, and especially of married women, is reflected in the increased participation of married women in the work-force outside the home. It should be noted that while there has been an increase in the participation of women in the labour-force outside the home, this does not mean that they are treated equally in employment. As Burke shows, the average industrial wage of women in Ireland in 1980 was only 69 per cent of that of their male counterparts.[9] Similar trends exist in other European countries. This has important implications for marriage, as earning power can also effect marital power.

The increasing contribution of women in industrial society is gaining acknowledgement which in turn is reflected in legislation such as the European Economic Community directive of 1971 on equal pay for women. Along with this acknowledgement, the acceptance of working mothers is also growing—as indicated by the provision of maternity leave, day nursery facilites and crèches. These changes help to contribute to the increased economic independence of women.

The movement towards the economic freedom of women in Western societies has been made possible by many factors, notably the effects of the two world wars. Women's labour was essential for the survival of most Western countries, especially for those countries engaged in the wars. Work that was previously the preserve of men, such as heavy industrial work, had to be done by women, as men were required for the armies. Changes in working practices have been hastened by the decrease in the importance of physical strength for many unskilled and semi-skilled jobs. The development of home aids such as washing machines and the electric power to drive them, and the ready availability of prepared foods such as bread and frozen goods, have also been significant. They have helped to free the housewife from many household tasks that previously consumed much of her time. This has helped to make it possible for a family to have both partners in a marriage employed outside the home. The economic position of women has been further changed by the shift from a production-orientated to a consumption-orientated economy.[10]

Crucial to the exercise of this economic freedom is the control modern woman has over her reproductive function. Without reliable birth control the attainment of economic freedom would be almost impossible. Although the effects of contraception are discussed primarily in the context of gender equality, the consequences of this technological advance pervades all the changes discussed in this chapter.

The effects of economic freedom on marriage are enormous. Probably the most dramatic effect has been to give individuals the freedom to choose to stay with or to leave their marital partners. Without the economic developments of this century, couples would have little choice concerning whether or not to stay together. Previously, they had virtually no economic alternatives. As Bernard puts it, "Liberation means choice among alternatives."[11]

Apart from legal and moral restrictions, many couples in Western society can now choose whether or not to stay together. Economic necessity no longer controls their decision. Landis and Landis summed up the situation when they wrote: "Although some utilitarian reasons for marriage have been minimized by technological and social changes, the basic needs that impel people towards monogamous marriage remain unchanged. In fact the very changes that have decreased the power of external controls on marriage stability have given greater force to the affectional function of marriage."[12]

It should be noted that the economic alternative to marriage for many married women is not always an attractive one, especially for those who have children. For example, in Britain almost half of the fatherless families in the National Child Development Study were dependent on State benefits during some time. One in six were dependent on the State as their only souce of income.[13] In the United States nearly 60% of all children born in 1986 will spend part of their lives in a single-parent home before the age of 18 with the most common problem for single-parent mothers being economic.[14] The argument here is not that the economic alternatives for married women are equally good, but that the alternatives do exist, however unattractive they may be. It is the presence of these alternatives that makes it no longer always necessary for wives to stay in marriage purely for economic reasons.

Related to the economic changes for women, are

changed attitudes to the roles of the sexes which are reflected in the movement towards gender equality.

Holter's examination of sex roles[15] leads her to conclude: "the sociological, anthropological and social-psychological theories all seem to point 'ultimately' to changes in the requirements of the economic system as the prime moving force of shifts in sex roles or changes in the status of women."[16]

Whatever the cause of change, there is general agreement that marked changes in attitudes towards the position of women have occurred. Examples of these changes include women's suffrage, equal pay, and greater opportunity of employment.

Although women are still grossly discriminated against, discrimination appears at least to be decreasing. Women still have a long way to go before achieving liberation from the domination of men, but male domination is at least being seriously challenged. The impact of this challenge has been felt in most areas of social life, including marriage.

In spite of this challenge to male domination, children even up to present times are still socialized to accept difference in the sexes that have no biological base. Generally, girls are given dolls to play with, and boys are given cars. It is still a violation of propriety for either sex to do what is customarily reserved for the other. Men and women are not free to choose whatever job they want, using only the criterion of efficiency, convenience and capacity. Some men still object to women taking over high-level jobs just as they object to men undertaking women's tasks.[17]

While these attitudes still prevail, there has been an interesting change. In many countries up to recently women were prohibited by law from taking up certain types of prestigious work. As Goode observes, if women really could not do various kinds of male tasks, no moral or external prohibition would be necessary to keep them from these tasks.[18] The change that has occurred is almost the reverse of this. Many Western countries now have legislation which prevents discriminatory employment practices based on sex. Women, once defined by law as inferior, are now being defined as equal. Men, who may be slow to relinquish their position of dominance, are increasingly being confronted by women who are no longer seeing themselves as less than equal.

An interesting aspect of changing perspectives on women can be found in a comparison between attitudes prevalent in Western industrial countries and those held in some socialist countries. In the West women have yet to obtain equality in society, while within marriage the relationship between the sexes is increasingly becoming egalitarian. In socialist countries equality in society, has been obtained at least theoretically, but marriages still continue to reflect more traditional attitudes.

The comparison suggests that changes in marriage are not always reflected in society; nor are attitudinal changes in society necessarily transferred to marriage. It seems likely, however, that insofar as marriage is a microcosm of male-female relationships, the move towards egalitarianism in Western marriage most likely reflects a general change in attitudes towards women. While gender-related attitudes have become more flexible, research shows that sterotypes about the sexes have shown few changes over the past 40 years.[19]

To suggest, however, that the movement towards an egalitarian society in the West reflects acceptance of gender equality is not necessarily correct. For example, the low status and low pay of women in employment relative to men poses a serious challenge to the equality argument. The movement toward egalitarianism simply illustrates, according to Holter, a tendency to increase women's influence in institutions that are decreasing in importance as social and political units. Furthermore, she describes the changes as mainly a trend towards latent sex discrimination as opposed to manifest discrimination in traditional societies. This covert discrimination she calls "quasi/egalitarianism" on the basis that present day sexual discrimination is neither officially accepted nor manifested in legal codes and thus constitutes a contrast to the official ideology of most Western countries. This points to a discrepancy between ideology and reality.[20]

Whatever the arguments about present-day trends in changing attitudes between the sexes, men and women approach each other in marriage on a different basis. The traditional Christian marriage ceremony joined the couple together with a quotation from the New Testament exhorting husbands to love their wives, and wives to obey their husbands. Couples entering marriage with this sentiment were unlikely to have come together as equals. Today they come to marriage at least professing to be two equal persons. They see their sexual differences as complementary, and each expects to attain fuller development as individuals. Increasingly few men expect their prospective wives to obey them and fewer women are willing to accede to their demands. The bond that attracts and unites the couple in marriage is becoming more and more based on notions of romantic love and the acceptance of each other as equals.

Finally, let us examine the effect on marriage of changed attitudes to sex. The sexual freedom of post-World War II industrial societies is in sharp contrast to the puritanical attitudes of the Victorian era. Many of the old taboos surrounding sex seem to be waning. This is illustrated by public displays of affection which go without comment because they have become an acceptable part of everyday life; the acceptance of pregnancy outside of marriage as reflected in the increase of "caring services" for unmarried parents; and the introduction of sex education in the school curriculum. Sex is increasingly seen as a normal part of human functioning, no longer clouded in mystery or talked about only by implication. The changes in attitudes towards sex during this century have been so great that many writers have described the changes as a sexual revolution.[21]

Although there has been a definite change in attitudes towards sex, the change has not necessarily resulted in an increase in casual sexual relations. The preponderance of research evidence shows that the change, rather than giving rise to indiscriminate casual sexual relations, has in fact, given rise to an increased association between sex and commitment.[22]

As far back as 1965, Schofield in his extensive study of the sexual behaviour of young people in Great Britain, concluded that the vast majority of his respondents engaged in sexual activity only with partners with whom they had a continuous relationship.[23] Gorer was led to the conclusion from his study of a sample of 1,791 that, despite the impression given by the contemporary mass communications with all its emphasis on the permissive society, only one quarter of the male respondents and one thirtieth of the female respondents could possibly be accurately labelled with the journalistic phrase "permissive."[24]

Reiss from his research on sexual attitudes in the United States found little evidence to show an increase in the popularity of sex without affection.[25] Macklin, in her extensive review of research on extramarital sex, concluded that the majority of people in the surveys reported an emotional involvement with their partners.[26] From the various research findings it seems that changes in attitudes towards sex have resulted in a more open acceptance and acknowledgement of sexual behaviour with an increased association between love and sex.

These changes in attitudes towards sex are also reflected in marriage. Wives no longer "submit"to the sexual demands of their husbands out of duty. In fact, there has almost been a reversal of that situation in that husbands are becoming as much concerned about satisfying their wives' sexual demands as wives are about having them met. Both men and women are seeing sexual fulfilment as normal, and both expect this fulfilment in marriage. Melville, in his review of research findings on marital sexuality in the United States, concluded that the studies show that sex has become a more mutually enjoyable experience in marriage.[27] Gorer found in England that only 2 per cent of the men and 4 per cent of the women considered sexual love not very important in marriage, with 1 percent of both sexes considering it not at all important.[28]

In discussing changing attitudes towards sex it is important to distinguish sexual fulfilment in marriage from eroticism. Contrary to Shorter's thesis that there was a stripping away of the sentimental layers of the romantic experience in the 1950s and the 1960s to get at a hard "sexual core,"[29] research findings as indicated above tend to show an increase in the association between love and sex. There is no evidence to support the popular belief that there is widespread use of such practices as "swinging" (spouse swapping) and other similar attempts to dissociate love and sex. Macklin estimated that about 2 per cent of the U. S. adult population engaged in swinging. This estimate is based on studies from the early 1970s as there is no recent information. This, she suggests, might reflect a "fading of a fad."[30] Hunt on the basis of his research also found that relatively few people managed to make permissive marriage (that is a marriage that includes extra-marital erotic satisfactions such as swinging) work at all, let alone exclusive marriage ... since for most people sex is closely bound up with deep emotions.[31]

Mutual sexual gratification in modern marriage may not always be achieved, but it certainly seems to be held as an ideal. The association of love and sex is increasingly becoming a feature of modern marriage. Although Winch concludes his analysis of research findings on love and sex in America by stating that they are more closely associated by women than by men, and by middle-class more than by lower-class,[32]

Komarovsky's classic study of blue collar marriage found that only a small minority of the families studied fit the familiar stereotype of the virile but insensitive working-class husband and his long-suffering wife who grimly performs her sexual duty.[33]

Undoubtedly the increased availability of effective contraception, although in part a result of changing attitudes towards sex, has also been a contributor. The main effect of contraception has been the separation of sex and reproduction. This separation and its practice in marriage challenges procreation as a primary function of marriage. Now in Western marriage, the personal fulfilment of the spouses can take equal or even higher status over the procreative function.

By separating sex and reproduction, contraception enables couples to plan the number of children they want. The result is the reduction in family size that is evident from the census figures of most industrial countries. In addition, the reasons for having children have become more child-centred. For example, children are no longer seen as reflecting the virility of the parents, but are generally conceived only if the parents feel that they can provide the maximum opportunity for their children's individual growth and development.

In the context of marriage the effects of changing attitudes towards sex have been many The expectation of full sexual achievement may be viewed as a great new liberation for couples. However, these changes are not without their difficulties, and not least among these is the disillusionment that results from failure to achieve this sexual bliss, a failure that is often directly related to the expectation of its achievement.

What we see then from these various changes is the evolution of a concept of marriage based on companionship. Central to this companionship is the notion of personal fulfilment within a relationship where a person's basic human need for emotional understanding and support is met. This friendship dimension, as it were, is growing in importance and the achievement of this friendship is becoming more crucial to a happy relationship.

The social changes discussed in this chapter have all contributed to the development of this ideal of friendship in marriage. The increased economic independence of married women has added the element of choice, an essential ingredient of any friendship relationship. Notions of equality in marriage are a natural consequence of the women's liberation movement and expectations of sexual fulfilment must be, in part at least, affected by the sexual revolution of this century and the availability of effective means of contraception.

Companionship is by no means new to marriage. What is new is its importance. With the reduction in functions performed by marriage and the family, those that are left have taken on an increased significance. It is logical to assume that the more marriage becomes based on companionship, the greater the risk of collapse when the companionship or affectional needs are not being met.

For the therapist the crucial question arising out of this must surely be to ask where the roots of the couple's unhappiness lie. The answer, obviously, will depend on the circumstances involved for each individual couple. If the unhappiness is due to changed expectations of marriage as a result of changes in society, then the approach to marital therapy must reflect this.

A framework for marital therapy which takes account of these changing expectations is presented in the next chapter. It is based on the distinct notions of companionship and institutional marriage. By identifying a couple's tendency towards either of these two types, and the degree of harmony that exists between their consequent role expectations, a framework for analysis that takes account of the impact of social change on their marriage is provided.

NOTES

1. The family is included with marriage in this chapter, but references to the family will be restricted to those aspects where the change has resulting major effects on the marriage relationship.

2. The terms "companionship" and "institutional" are taken from E. Burgess, H. Locke and M. Thomes, *op. cit*. They are often used interchangeably with "modern" and "traditional" respectively.

3. W. Ogburn and N. Nimkoff, *A Handbook of Sociology*, 5th ed. (London 1964), p. 488.

4. T. Parsons and R. Bales, *Family, Socialization and the Interaction Process* (London 1956), p. 16.

5. R. Coser, *The Family: Its Structure and Functions* (New York 1964), p. xxviii.

6. Notions of family functions are derived from a functionalist approach in Sociology. For a critical discussion see C. C. Harris *The Family and Industrial Society* (London 1983).

7. T. Parsons and R. Bales, *op. cit.* , p.9.

8. *Ibid.* pp. 24-5.

9. H. Burke, "Continunity and Change: The Life Cycle of Irish Women in the 1980s" in *The Changing Family* ed. Family Studies Unit (Dublin 1984).

10. H. Holter, "Sex Roles and Social Change," in *Family, Marriage, and the Struggle of the Sexes*, H. Dreitzel, ed. (New York 1972), p. 159.

11. J. Bernard, *The Future of Marriage* (Harmondsworth 1976), p. 230.

12. J. Landis and M. Landis, *Building a Successful Marriage* , 5th ed. (New Jersey 1968), p. 8.

13. E. Ferri, *Growing Up in a One-Parent Family* (London 1976)

14. E. Macklin "Nontraditional Family Forms" in M. Sussman and S. Steinmetz, eds. *Handbook of Marriage and the Family* (New York 1987), p. 328.

15. The term "role" is used as it implies a differentiation between biology and culture.

16. H. Holter, *op. cit.*, p.154.

17. W. Goode, *The Family* (New Jersey 1964), p. 70.

18. *Ibid*.

19. S. Losh-Hesselbart "Development of Gender Roles" in M. Sussman and S. Steinmetz *op.cit.* p.541.

20. H. Holter, *op. cit.*, p. 161. This discrepancy between ideology and reality is similar to that suggested for socialist countries earlier in the text.

21. See E. Shorter, *op. cit.*, p. 78, and A. Skolnick, *The Intimate Environment* (Boston 1973), p. 188.

22. M. Lamanna and A. Riedman, *Marriage and Families*, 2nd ed. (Belmont 1983), Chapter 13.

23. M. Schofield, *The Sexual Behaviour of Young People* (London 1965), p. 253.

24. G. Gorer *Sex and Marriage in England Today* (St Albans Herts 1973), pp. 47-57.

25 I. Reiss, *The Family Systems in America* (New York 1971), p. 159.

26. E. Macklin, *op. cit.*, p. 332.

27. K. Melville, *Marriage and Family Today* (New York 1977), p. 272.

28. G. Gorer, *op. cit.*, p. 147.

29. E. Shorter, *op. cit.*, p. 79.

30. E. Macklin, *op. cit.*, p. 334.

31. M. Hunt, *Sexual Behavior in the 1970s* (New York 1974), p. 240.

32. R. Winch, *op. cit.*, pp. 318-19.

33. M. Komarovsky, *Blue Collar Marriage* (New York 1962), p. 82.

Chapter 4

Compatibility in Marriage

"We are just not compatible," is often the final exasperated declaration by couples when they feel that their relationship is coming to an end. There is something seemingly indisputable about this type of statement, so much so, that in many countries it constitutes legal grounds for divorce. But what people mean by this lack of compatibility is often not very clear. It can have different meanings for different people. For many, however, it is an expression of the pain and frustration they feel in the relationship, but the cause of which they somehow cannot seem to pin-point.

Compatibility emcompasses many things. It can include having the same likes and dislikes, sharing a value system, and generally having similar attitudes towards the world. Compatibility can also include a match between contrasts such as that between a dominant and a less dominant person. Social and personal needs also play a part with, for example, the status satisfaction we derive from association with a person who has characteristics we admire. In addition to all of these, there are the expectations we have of our partner. These expectations have to do with how we think each partner should perform their role in the relationship. Expectations play a major part in any couple's compatibility. They are seldom explicit, and for many never fixed. For this reason these role expectations can be a source of much unhappiness and frustration for many couples.

Take, for example, the case of Janie and Bob who came seeking marital therapy because they felt they were growing apart emotionally. Janie complained that Bob did not express his love for her and that she felt taken for granted by him. Bob replied that in his view Janie should know that he loves her without his having to tell her by saying "I love you" or by buying flowers or performing other similar actions that are seen as expressions of love. Such expressions he called unmanly and, anyway, he would hardly be married to her if he did not love her. She would reply, "Then why don't you show me?"

What Janie and Bob's difficulty reflects is two people with different expectations about the expression of feelings in a relationship.[1] Janie would like them freely and openly expressed and thus shared. Bob sees them as intrinsic to the marriage and not requiring such expression. Taking this difference in their expectations, a role compatibility continuum can be constructed. On such a continuum, Janie and Bob would appear on opposite ends with regard to the exchange of feelings. By applying this measure to others, any couple's interaction can be plotted on the continuum. Those who have little expectation of the type of emotional exchange desired by Janie are placed on the same side as Bob, while those who have a high expectation are placed on the other side with Janie.

The continuum can be expanded to include other

areas of role compatibility around the theme of expectations, as further illustrated by Janie and Bob's situation.

Continuing to give an explanation of their difficulties, Bob said that he felt that Janie did not give him credit for all that he did in the marriage. When he compared himself to other husbands he felt that he came out quite well because not only did he maintain a steady job, but he also helped with housework, cared for the children and sometimes babysat so that Janie could have some time for herself. Many of his "husband" friends did not do all of these things and none that he knew helped their wives as much around the house. He hastened to add, however, that these remarks were not intended as complaints but merely noted to explain his bewilderment with Janie's unhappiness with him as a husband. For Janie, these very comparisons, so important it seemed to him, were a basic source of emotional distance. Why, she pleaded, can't he relate to me on the basis of my individuality, my uniqueness, and not by some general norm he applies to the universality of "wives?" Here, again, we find them on opposite ends of the continuum, Bob applying generalized expectations to Janie as a wife and to himself as a husband, while Janie wants them to relate simply as Janie and Bob, unique and individual.

A third area of difference between Janie and Bob arises out of this and has to do with the performance of tasks. Janie felt that she could be replaced by a maid, cook and concubine, as she felt that Bob was concerned only with how well she performed these and other roles and that there was little if any appreciation by him of her as a person. Bob could happily be married to a robot as far as she was concerned. Bob, however, did not agree with Janie, yet he continued to focus on these various tasks, and used them as criteria in evaluating their respective roles in their marriage.

An interesting aspect of this tendency evident in Bob arises when one partner in the marriage equates performance of tasks with the demonstration of love. Take, for example, a wife who equates her husband's love for her with the jobs he does around the house. She is likely to feel unloved if he does not do them. This can be due to all kinds of situations with some of the most devastating arising in the case of inability to perform expected functions because of, for example, incapacity from accident or illness. In the event the husband's becoming unemployed in a marriage where task performance is equated with love, this loss of his provider role can be devastating. Illness and unemployment both lead to an inability to meet some task-performance expectations. Each presents its own crisis but when loss of love is associated with loss of task-performance then the couple are confronted by an additional crisis.

Returning to Janie and Bob, we see that in this area, too, they turned up on opposite ends of the continuum. Bob highly valued task-performance and equated this with his success as a wage earner and general handyman. Thus he saw himself as a "good husband." Janie continued to seek mutual recognition for their respective inherent qualities first and foremost as persons.

Finally, Janie and Bob's differences showed up

when Bob was asked if he shared his worries with Janie and he jokingly replied: "She is my wife, not my friend." While Bob may have said this in jest, the reality seems to have borne it out. For example, he felt that there were some aspects of his life, such as work-related tensions, that were more appropriately discussed with his workmates over a drink in the pub than with his wife. He justified this position by claiming genuinely that he did not want to worry Janie. She, however, would have preferred to be "worried" by his concerns as she felt excluded by him from part of his life because he did not share it with her. She believed she would be better able to deal with his occasional moodiness if she knew what was behind it.

Bob believed in maintaining a degree of separateness in their marriage, and he did not see it as appropriate to his role as husband/provider to share work matters with his wife. Janie, however, would have preferred more diffuse roles in their marriage within which they could relate to each other as friends, confidants, and emotional supporters, in addition to the roles of provider and housewife. Here again they turn up on opposite ends of the continuum.

Thus, the relationship between Janie and Bob when analysed on the basis of their role expectations shows them on opposite ends of the role compatibility continuum for each of the four areas identified. This is illustrated by Diagram I (p. 43).

DIAGRAM 1. ROLE COMPATIBILITY CONTINUUM

SHOWING POSITION OF JANIE AND BOB

Bob   Janie

I — — — — — — — — — — I

feelings kept to self	feelings shared
generalised standards	unique persons
tasks valued	individuals valued
specific roles	multiple roles

The diagram shows Janie on one end of the continuum with expectations that include the open expession of feelings, the acceptance of each other as unique persons, belief in being valued for oneself, and a desire to interact with Bob in multiple roles. At the other end of the continuum Bob expects to keep his feelings to himself, gauges marital behaviour by reference to other married couples, believes that spouses should value one another on the basis of how well tasks are performed and maintain a degree of separateness in their respective roles as husband and wife.

This classification is based only on role compatibility. However, other variables used to distinguish the two types of marriage, as identified in Chapter Three, could also be included on this continuum to give a more comprehensive listing of items under the headings of institutional and companionship marriage. For example, people tending towards institutional marriage are likely to place a high value on marriage itself as an institution. They will also tend to aproach the division of labour within marriage on the basis of sex, i.e. certain tasks will be seen as appropriate to a person by virtue of being male or female, such as house repairs being a husband's job, and laundry a wife's job. In addition, duty will be seen as a major bond in the relationship with rights and responsibilities vested in the respective roles of wife or husband, rather than in the person.

In contrast, companionship marriage is likely to place less emphasis on marriage as an institution and more on marriage as a relationship. Labour will tend to be divided on the basis of ability and interest, with less reliance on a division based on sex. Marriage bonds are likely to be based on affection, with rights and responsibilities negotiated from notions of equality. When these variables are combined with role compatibility, then a marriage continuum as represented in Diagram 2 (p. 45) emerges.

It should be noted, again, that these two types of marriage do not represent pure types. Neither can peoples' marriages necesarily be placed exclusively in one category or the other. For example, in some marriages, one partner might tend towards institutional marriage with the other tending towards companionship. Likewise, each partner might belong in a mix of categories, as for example, with a person who highly values the exchange of feelings in a relationship but also approaches the division of labour on the basis of sex roles. This is why it is described as a continuum with the various items grouped according to ideal types only.

DIAGRAM 2. ROLE COMPATIBILITY CONTINUUM

I ————————————— I

Institutional Marriage	Companionship Marriage
feelings kept to self	feelings shared
general standards applied	unique person
tasks valued	individual valued
specific roles	multiple roles
institution important	relationship important
labour divided by sex	labour divided by ability
bonds based on duty	affectional bonds
rights and responsibilities vested in role	negotiated rights and responsibilities

While taking account of these factors, the continuum can provide the marital therapist with a powerful diagnostic tool. By exploring with the couple the various items on the continuum, a picture of their role compatibility easily emerges. Thus, for example, if both partners were located as in Diagram 3 (p. 46) on the "companionship" side of the continuum they are likely to have compatible role expectations. The same would be true if they were both located on the "institutional" side of the continuum. If, however, they had different role expectations, as with the case of Janie and Bob, they would be located on opposite ends of the continuum as in Diagram 4 (p. 46).

DIAGRAM 3. ROLE COMPATIBILITY CONTINUUM
showing a couple with a high level of Role
Compatibility and a Companionship Marriage

I   _ _ _ _ _ _ _ _ _Husband_Wife I
Institutional   Companionship
Marriage   Marriage

DIAGRAM 4. ROLE COMPATIBILITY CONTINUUM
showing a couple with a low level of
Role Compatibility

I _Husband_ _ _ _ _ _ _ _Wife_ I
Institutional   Companionship
Marriage   Marriage

The plotting on the continuum is done by simply
evaluating each of the partner's expectations of
marriage by use of the variables described above. The
couple can be asked to give information about these
items in a way that is neither threatening nor
accusatory. One of the side benefits of using this
continuum is that it facilitates couples sharing
information about their relationship in a way that does
not imply blame. Neither end of the continuum is in
itself better or worse than the other. They are simply
different. The difference, however, is of such

importance, that for many couples this process can give them an understanding of their interaction that enables them to set about bridging the emotional gap that has caused so much hurt and frustration.

As a framework for analysis, the continuum takes account of the impact of social change on marriage on a systemic level as represented by the evolution of companionship marriage. In addition, it takes account of this social change on an individual level by allowing each person in the marriage to be located separately on the continuum.[2] Positions are not fixed, and as new influences come to bear on either partner, change can result.

Marriages are constantly in a state of change. Sometimes the change leads to growth in the relationship, at other times it leads to tension, as illustrated by the role compatibility continuum. The effect of the change is determined by the way each partner in the relationship reacts to it. When the change is accommodated, it is likely to lead to growth. When it is not, tension arises. For example, some people in marriage react with aggression that manifests itself as physical violence. Others react with depression or physical illnesses and end up as patients at the local clinic. On the other hand, some couples will adapt to change spontaneously as people do to other changes in life.

The key to successfully accommodating change other than spontaneously, is, first, to recognise the change. This may seem self-evident but many couples see the "symptom," such as the alcoholism, the depression, the extra-marital affair or whatever, as the cause of their difficulties rather than as the result of change, which is frequently the case. By recognising the changes and defining their difficulties in the context of these changes, the couple prepare themselves to begin to resolve them. It must be emphasized that people are not always aware of the influence of society on them, and therefore are not always aware of the changes that have occurred. What a person might have been quite happy with in the past can easily become a source of great frustration in the future. A very clear example of this is found in the changing of roles of men and women in society and the spin-off effect of this on marriage relationships. Accommodating change in marriage is primarily a matter or re-negotiation which begins with the conscious recognition that change has occurred.

NOTES

1. The classification that follows is based on Parson's pattern variables which were developed from Tonnies's two basic categories of social relationships called in German sociological literature, *"geminschaft"* and *"gesellschaft."* See T. Parsons *The Structure of Social Action*, 2nd ed. (New York 1949), pp. 686-94.

2. The continuum incorporates change on a macro-systemic level as well as a micro-level.

Chapter 5

Specialization in Marriage

The main theoretical concepts underpinning
Reinvestment Therapy and the Role Compatibility
Continuum are for use with couples whose
unhappiness in marriage is primarily due to the impact
on their marriage of changes in society. The concepts
are drawn from systems theory and incorporate
aspects of Parsons's general theory of action.[1] In this
context, marriage is seen as a dynamic social system
interacting with other social systems within the wider
society and all the systems influencing the others.

The notion of system is widespread in modern
society. We find it in use everywhere: communication
systems; banking systems; systems of government;
even the gambler has a system. Generally the term
"system" is used to describe some set of relationships,
or a way in which something is organized. It is the
totality of a particular set of relationships and
interactions, with all behaviours fitting together in a
mutually influencing process. Everything within the
system has a meaning and the context of any part of the
system is its relationship to the other parts and to the
system as a whole. Thus, when we refer to marriage
and society as systems, their interaction and
interdependence become easily apparent.

Social systems theory has received much attention in the past few decades in the fields of applied behavioural sciences.[2] For example, in social work it has been used as a theoretical framework for the development of a unitary approach to social work methods.[3] As an orientation for the psychotherapist, it has many significant insights to offer, especially for those involved in working directly with social systems as distinct from personality systems.

According to Buckley a system is a whole which functions as a whole by virtue of the interdependence of its parts. General systems theory is the study of the way the parts are interrelated. Whether the systems are living or non-living, they are governed by some of the same basic laws. Human social aggregates referred to as social systems exhibit all the features of organized systems. Social systems theory is the conceptual framework used for the study of how these social systems are maintained or changed.[4]

It is perhaps more accurate to talk about system theories as there are several different models.[5] The one used here is what Buckley, its chief exponent, calls a process model of systems theory.[6] This model places emphasis on the importance of change.[7] Here systems are seen as self-regulating, directing and organizing.[8] As such, they do not merely react to stimuli, but are intrinsically active themselves. This orientation to systems is based on the principle that the person is an active personality capable of self-initiated behaviour.[9] Buckley calls this process morphogenesis and defines it as "those processes which tend to elaborate or change a system's given form, structure or state."[10] As Goldstein points out, the use of this model "assigns to the system the potential to achieve a higher order of problem solving and the capacity to grow, learn and change."[11]

Essentially, then, the process model of systems theory maintains that marriage, like other social systems, evolves in response both to changes that occur in society (i.e. the system's environment) and to changes initiated from within marriage itself. This evolution can be seen in the effect on marriage of such changes as the increased economic freedom of women and the movement towards gender equality and changes brought about internally by alterations in the partners' expectations of each other.

Marriage, as a social system, therefore, is seen as a dynamic, interacting unit evolving in response to new needs and new demands. This evolutionary change is what Parsons describes as change that enhances a system's adaptive capacity. From this perspective change is seen as consisting of a double process. The first is a process of differentiation whereby parts of a system divide and separate from each other forming new sub-systems. The second process results from this and consists of the development of new sources for the performance of the specialized functions of the new sub-system.[12]

In the context of marriage in Western society, the first process of differentiation can be seen with the transfer of some of the functions of marriage to other social systems, as discussed in Chapter Three (for example, the educational function which has been given to schools, and the economic function to places of employment outside the home and in some cases to the state through welfare programmes). Because this process of transferring functions to other social systems is evolutionary, modern marriage should, as a result, have an increased capacity for fulfilling the functions that are left. Essentially this means that with few functions to perform, modern marriage should be more specialized and consequently better equipped to fulfill the remaining functions. Since a primary function left is the meeting of affectional needs, as discussed in Chapter Three, it should therefore be better able to meet the individual partners' needs for affection. Marriage is thus becoming a specialized institution for the meeting of affectional needs.

What then are the sources in marriage today for meeting affectional needs since this has become a specialized function? In the past, ascription often served as a major source. In other words, a couple simply by being in the role of husband and wife invested affection in the relationship. Love for the other person was assumed to be part of the role, just as authority is assumed to be part of a police officer's role, and knowledge of engines to be part of a mechanic's. To a large extent, ascription as a source for affection worked fine when marriage and the family had many functions. It often worked well in institutional marriage because of its many functions. In companionship marriage, however, with its increased specialization resulting from differentiation, the giving and receiving of affection can no longer be assumed to follow simply because a man and a woman hold the position of husband and wife.

The couple need to find new sources for the fulfilling of their affectional needs. It is this quest for new sources for affection that seems to be the crux of companionship marriage. Those who find new sources are likely to continue develping their relationships. Those who don't are likely to end the relationship or at best to continue in an unfulfilled one.

When two people, however, desire a relationship with each other and have the same expectations of marriage, there would seem to be a relatively high possibility of finding the sources for affection. The problem is more likely to arise when they have different expectations with one of them tending towards companionship marriage while the other partner's expectations are more in line with institutional marriage.

Reinvestment Therapy was designed specifically for use with couples such as Bob and Janie. Their difficulties were largely due to changes in their expectations of each other. These expectations had been influenced by changes in the wider society. The differences between Janie and Bob, although manifested on an individual level, were as much a reflection of what was going on in their environment as what was experienced by them privately. Here social change and individual change were finding their expression in a changed relationship.

NOTES

1. Parsons, *op. cit.*.

2. For examples of its use in the fields of the behavioural sciences see W. Bennis, K. Benne and R. Chin, eds *The Planning of Change* (New York 1961), pp. 201-14; G. Hearn, ed., *The General Systems Approach* (New York 1969); M. Janchill, "Systems Concepts in Casework Theory and Practice," *Social Casework* 50 (No. 2, 1969), pp. 74-82; R. Lippit, J. Watson and B. Westley, *Dynamics of Planned Change* (New York 1958); J. Monane, *A Sociology of Human Systems* (New York 1967) and P. Barker, *Basic Family Therapy* (London 1981).

3. The use of general systems theory for this purpose in social work can be found in H. Goldstein, *Social Work Practice: A Unitary Approach* (Columbia 1973); H. Specht, and A. Vickery, *Integrating Social Work Methods* (London 1977) and M. Heus and A. Pincus *The Creative Generalist: A Guide to Social Work Practice* (Barneveld Wisconsin 1986).

4. W. Buckley, *Modern Systems Reseach for the Behavioural Scientist* (Chicago 1968), p. xvii.

5. See, W. Buckley, *Sociology and Modern Systems Theory* (New Jersey 1967).

6. *Ibid* , p. 18.

7. Much of the criticism of the use of systems theory in the applied fields, especially social work, seems to have failed to recognize this point and the fact that there are different models of systems theory.

8. W. Buckley, *op. cit.*, p. 58.

9. This principle is gaining increasing importance in psychology as reflected in Gestalt Psychology and the work of Piaget and Rogers.

10. W. Buckley, *op. cit.*, p. 58.

11. H. Goldstein, *op. cit.*, p. 117.

12. T. Parsons, *Societies: Evolutionary and Comparative Perspectives* (New Jersey 1966), pp. 21-2. Differentiation and integration are processes discussed by Parsons in relation to a system's dynamics. They are used here with a somewhat different meaning than that used by Parsons.

Chapter 6

Reinvestment Therapy Explained

Reinvestment Therapy is intended for use with those couples who are experiencing marital unhappiness primarily as a result of social change. Essentially these are couples who are having difficulty because of a transition from institutional to companionship marriage and who often find themselves on different sides of the role compatibility continuum, as explained in Chapter Four. This can be due either to the partners' different orientation towards marriage as expressed by these two types of relationship, or to their struggle as a couple to attain a shared orientation.

The basic premise underlying Reinvestment Therapy is that relationships tend to be happy when the partners are able to meet each other's affectional needs. Working from this premise, therapy becomes the development of mutual feelings of caring between the spouses. Success in attaining these feelings results in increased mutual satisfaction. This success is achieved when couples are able to find sufficent sources in their relationship for the meeting of their affectional needs. It is this task of expanding and finding sources of affection that forms the core element of this approach to therapy. It requires reinvestment in the relationship by the partners. The emphasis on reinvestment in the relationship is crucial. It is not sufficient for people simply to want the marriage. They must want and be prepared to seek actively an expansion of the relationship with each other.

Not all couples can do this. Some may have grown too far apart to be able to make such a reinvestment. The risk of further pain from possible disappointment might be too great. Others might lack an ability to be intimate or might be in need of some other form of help before being able to work on re-building their marriage. Barriers to reinvestment, such as alcoholism, could also be present. Reinvestment Therapy assumes an ability and an openness to reinvesting emotionally in one another. It is only with this openness that the couple can be engaged in finding new sources of affection and the expansion of those that already exist.

There are three main phases in Reinvestment Therapy. These are the engagement phase, the exploration phase, and the consolidation phase. The first of these, the engagement phase, is focused on engaging the couple in therapy. The exploration phase is concerned with helping the couple to explore new sources of affection in their relationship. The last phase, the consolidation phase, is centred on helping the couple to consolidate new ways of interaction developed during the exploration phase. Although these phases overlap in practice, they are described as three distinct phases simply for the purpose of presentation. Their description here is broad with the intent of providing an overview of the approach. Some of the detail is continued in subsequent chapters.

The first phase, the engagement phase, is essentially concerned with motivating the couple to become involved in the therapy. It is not just an evaluation of their desire for a more satisfying relationship. The phase has definite psychotherapeutic objectives. These objectives follow in a sequence beginning with the first session and culminating with the couple's engagement in therapy. The title "engagement phase" is used not only because the objective is the engagement of the couple in therapy, but also because the word "engagement," being the word used to describe the period of courtship before relationship, conveys the ideas relevant to this phase. Engagement before relationship is a period of testing, sharing, apprehension, excitement and commitment. This first phase of the therapy shares these characteristics.

The first interview is always a joint interview, that is, an interview in which the two partners are seen together. The importance of seeing both partners together at the outset cannot be overemphasized. Reinvestment Therapy is essentially the process of enabling two people to effect change in their interaction. It is not the treatment of individuals who are married. Seeing the partners separately can be counter-productive if the intended focus of the therapy is the couple's interaction. The interaction cannot be observed if only one person is present. An individual's reporting of the interaction is their perception of it, as experienced by them, and cannot be relied upon as objective. The partners in the relationship can only report the interaction as they separately experience it, a process that by its very nature is subjective. Thus the need to be able to observe the interaction.

There are many additional benefits from the use of a joint interview for the first session. If it is insisted that both partners be present for the first session, the couple are made to do something about their relationship before coming: that is, they must agree to come together and be present with each other while discussing their relationship. This insistence can test motivation. It also prevents the therapist from being trapped into seeing only one partner for a number of sessions before attempting to engage the other. This trap creates many difficulties. For example, the spouse who is seen second is likely to come with feelings generated from knowing that the other spouse has already discussed the relationship, and will probably relate to the therapist on the basis of these feelings. This can be reflected in such ways as the second partner guessing what the first partner has said and trying to respond to this; or feeling the need to defend him or herself; or expecting the therapist to have already taken sides. A joint session at the outset eliminates most of these difficulties.

Phase one begins with a highly structured joint session directed towards achievement of specific objectives. The first objective is to have each partner listen to the other's perception of the relationship and their major areas of dissatisfaction. The session revolves around this exchange. It provides the major information on the couple. Apart from sharing their perceptions, the couple also manifest something about their own interaction, communication patterns, and knowledge of each other that provide entry points for the therapist. By the end of the session, each spouse should have achieved the therapeutic objective of an increased knowledge of the relationship. This growth in knowledge is the result of being helped to listen to one another and of becoming more aware of existing patterns of interaction.

The achievement of the objectives of the first session should advance feelings of being understood, which in turn have the effect of reducing anxiety and enhancing hope. This does not necessarily mean that either or both of the partners will feel less discomfort or that any change in the relationship will result. The effect is somewhat similar to that of insight development.

In helping the couple to listen to each other, the therapist must play an active part. It is unlikely that a couple who are experiencing a high level of conflict will be able to permit each other equal time during a first session. Neither will they be able to share undefensively a perspective on the relationship. To help the couple with this, the therapist may need to introduce ground rules for the session and, depending on the level of conflict, may even need to make acceptance of these rules a condition for therapy. These rules will depend on the nature of the situation. For example, where one partner interrupts to the extent of preventing the other from sharing, the therapist might stop interruptions by making a rule that each must listen to the other without interjecting. To facilitate involvement in the session it is sometimes useful to introduce some more general rules such as asking that the partners do not afterwards make each other defend what has been said during the session. The obvious reason for this type of control is that unless it is made explicit, it is likely that only material that can be defended will be shared. It is important to allow natural and spontaneous interaction, but this interaction also needs controls if it is to be helpful.

Uncontrolled interaction when conflict is high is generally only destructive.

Once the therapist has achieved the first objective of enabling the couple to listen to each other, attention is then focused on examining their commitment to working on their relationship. Essentially this involves discovering the willingness of each partner to change. It frequently happens that couples seeking help with their relationship approach such help in the abstract. That is, they might see change in the relationship as something outside themselves, or at best as change in the other spouse to which they are willing to react positively. This vague positive reaction is often the extent of the individual commitment to change. To accept this concept of change as a starting-point in therapy is tantamount to accepting no commitment at all, irrespective of how vehemently it may be pronounced. Commitment like this has the effect of removing responsibility for change from the couple. The result is that change is expected to emerge from the therapy sessions and attendance at these sessions is assumed to be all that is needed. Somehow, coming to the sessions and talking about the marriage is assumed to be a process that will "mysteriously" bring about change in the relationship. It is only when individual responsibility for change is accepted that the couple can meaningfully invest themselves in a change process that transcends the therapy sessions. It is all too easy and indeed common to project the cause of one's discomfort in a relationship on to the "relationship"as if it were something apart from the two people that constitute it.

Although some history in the form of background

information is collected during the engagement phase, history-taking is not a primary task. Background information is collected throughout the therapy process in all three phases. No attempt is made to collect an exhaustive or comprehensive history of the couple either as individuals or as a partners. Information only directly relevant to the situation at hand is collected. Thus, information is collected only if it enhances understanding or facilitates participation in the current exchange. For example, asking a couple about an earlier period in their relationship could be for the purpose of understanding more about the development of their relationship over time, or it could be to introduce a more neutral area of discussion in order to relieve tension. The therapist might even decide at times not to ask about aspects of their history as this might have a specific therapeutic advantage at a later time. Also, the answer given to an inquiry about past events will be affected by the "now" feelings of the couple. For example, a person in a relationship which now produces great discomfort is likely either to block out memories of past pleasant experiences or to exaggerate them.

This phase is completed when the couple are engaged in therapy, that is, an engagement which involves a commitment to changing themselves. To facilitate this engagement, the therapist is explicit about what will be expected of the couple when they are engaging in therapy. A verbal contract should be established, outlining such items as expected duration of therapy in both number of sessions and time. The length and frequency of sessions, a general guide to the form the sessions will take, and the explicit expectation on the part of the therapist that the couple will attempt to carry out the suggestions made, are also explained. This contract is formulated and agreed as soon as it is possible and in a manner that is helpful. This could be at the end of the first session, in parts over the phase, or at the end of the phase.

All sessions, and especially the first, end with the couple being assigned a task to perform before the next session. The task is chosen on the basis of the information collected in that session, but usually should be of the nature of asking the individuals in the relationship to become more aware of themselves and of their effect on each other. The type of task assigned is directed towards the achievement of two primary objectives: getting both partners working on improving the relationship, and getting the focus of the individual to change on to his or herself and away from the other person.

This first phase can take from one to three sessions. If the phase extends much beyond three, the couple's expectations of therapy need to be re-evaluated. This could result in agreeing to terminate, or to seek other objectives apart from increasing mutual satisfaction. These new objectives could involve providing supportive counselling, referral to another service, or separation counselling. It is likely that if a couple require more than the three sessions to become engaged in the therapy that they either need a different service, or are not ready to use therapy at this time.

The exploration phase, which is the second phase of the therapy process, can be one of great excitement for the couple as they explore themselves and each other. The exploration can lead to a new freedom in the relationship, a freedom that is characterised by feelings of personal fulfilment and the knowledge that happiness in their relationship can be a reality.[1] This reality is made possible when the uniqueness and dignity of a human person is accepted and communicated by each partner to the other. With the translation of acceptance into action, the feelings of fulfilment seem boundless. Phase two, which is concerned with the search for and expansion of, sources of affection, has at its core this acceptance.

When the objectives of phase one have been achieved, phase two begins; this can be as early as the second session. However, it is not recommended that this phase should begin in the first session even if the objectives of phase one have been achieved. Time is an important factor and the couple can make best use of phase two if they have begun the process of change by carrying out the tasks assigned during phase one before becoming involved in phase two.

The couple enter phase two having already identified one or several problems that confront them in their relationship. Usually couples tend to emphasize one problem area or to seek to identify one problem area as the major source of conflict and dissatisfaction. The first objective in phase two is to help the couple to go beyond these problem areas. Substantially this involves having them explore feelings in their relationship non-judgmentally. This exploration is difficult for most couples because it involves confrontation with self, and learning new ways of interacting.

When couples begin this exploration it is usual for them to begin to feel that the relationship is worse than they originally thought. This feeling seems to be an unavoidable short-term effect for many couples when they honestly explore their feelings. The exploration brings to consciousness the often repressed feelings of loneliness and isolation felt in the relationship. Up to now, emotional energy had been spent on the conflicts. If these conflicts are temporarily removed, even if only by such simple techniques as making them no-go areas, and the couple is then confronted with the deep, inner feelings generated by their relationship, the effect can be startling. Although the couple may feel that the relationship is worse than they feared and may experience great emotional pain because of this, they also feel a somewhat contradictory feeling of relief. The relief usually is associated with feelings of being understood by the therapist, combined with the knowledge that the areas of conflict can be left aside. Problems that were apparently insoluble become almost irrelevant. For example, it no longer seems to matter, at least for the time being, whether or not they feel love for one another.

This process begins during a joint session with the therapist asking the individual partners in the relationship if they feel cared for by each other. Whatever the reply, this exploration takes time and can even extend beyond one session. The initial question leads to examining such aspects of the couple's interaction as how caring is shown to each other, and what feeling cared for means to them individually. These feelings should necessarily avoid making judgment and should be expressed in a non-judgmental manner. For example, for me to say, "You do not understand me" is quite different to saying, "I do not feel understood." Both statements may contain the same meaning, but the first says something in the form of a judgment about you; the second says something about me.

This part of the process involves exploring a series of questions that go something like this: "I care for you;" "I think you feel cared for by me;" "What do I do to enable you to feel that I care?" and, "Do I think that you feel that I care for you?"If we examine this last question we see that it contains a number of interesting elements. For example, it keeps the responsibility in the first person; it emphasizes feeling and it implies no judgments. The question does not contain the words "ought"or "should." It is not sufficient to care; the caring must be demonstrated in a manner that ensures that the other person feels the caring.

Individuals with an institutional-type relationship, as described in Chapter Four, often identify the performance of tasks appropriate to a given role, such as the wife ironing her husband's shirts, as demonstrations of affection. In seeking new sources of affection they need to be helped to move beyond role performance as the criterion for measuring caring. Once they can do this, they begin to identify feelings of being understood as central to being cared for. At this point it is important to have the couple examine what they mean by being understood. This includes asking them what it would mean to them individually if they felt understood by each other. Couples usually respond to this examination by replying that to have such feelings of being understood by their partner would be equivalent to having achieved a degree of satisfaction in their relationship beyond their expectations. This expression becomes a new entry point in the therapeutic process.

The focus now becomes firmly established on the achievement of affectional needs. By this is meant the generation by the couple in each other of feelings of being cared for, understood, accepted, wanted and appreciated for what they are and how they are. The immediate result of this is the removal of all pressure on each other to change. For example, the husband is asked by the therapist to demonstrate caring for his wife, while at the same time asked not to expect her to modify any of her behaviour or to expect her to reciprocate with any demonstration of caring. She is asked to make the same commitment. Any change that occurs is thus the result of a personal decision rather than a result of giving in to the pressures from the other person in the relationship. For couples experiencing unhappiness this is often a new experience.

Some couples will have great difficulty in showing their caring for each other because of factors such as fear of being vulnerable if they leave their defensive positions. Such couples will need a lot of support, understanding and gentleness. Their experience of support from the therapist can be a primary enabling factor in helping them to take the risk of showing caring for each other. The therapist can enable them to begin reaching out to each other in the therapy session. Physical reaching out by the couples can be a useful preliminary to emotional reaching out. An example of this is having the couple sit close to one another and touch each other either by holding hands or by placing an arm around the other person. When the therapist is doing this with the couple it is important to be aware of the couple's feelings—such as embarrassment, fear of rejection, feeling silly, feeling relief, and when appropriate to help them to identify these feelings. Any expression of positive feelings should be focused on and allowed maximum experience.

In contrast to these couples, others will respond positively almost immediately. Frequently this immediate response is only an intellectual understanding. Either way the couple will need to experience this new freedom from pressure over time if it is to become the basis of a new pattern of interaction. To achieve this the couple will need to attempt to take pressure off each other, while at the same time reaching out emotionally between sessions. At first they may think it artificial, but even so, they should be encouraged. It can be difficult to try but once they take pressure off each other to change, they become, paradoxically, free to change.

The new motivation is based on a decision by the couple to show their caring for each other. From this the couple begin to define love in new terms. It is no longer seen as some vague sentiment or some undefinable feeling. Love becomes the decisions they individually make to enhance the fulfilment of one another.

The validity of this argument rests largely on the definition of affection already discussed in Chapter Two. If each partner can meet the affectional needs of the other, they will feel mutually fulfilled. Couples or individuals who claim to want the relationship to succeed but also say that they cannot meet these needs, should be helped to examine what they mean by wanting the relationship to "succeed." Sometimes when this happens, the individuals concerned are often referring to the relationship as some abstraction outside of the personal relationship, that requires no self-investment.

The establishment of a new contract is the final task of phase two. The new contract is based on the "now experiences" of the couple and as such the contract usually has developed throughout this phase. It is only if the contract has not already been agreed that it is necessary to make a new one at the end of the phase. The new contract involves shifting the goal of therapy to the meeting of affectional needs and away, temporarily at least, from the resolution of the problems that have presented themselves.

As indicated already, phase two can begin anywhere from the second to the fourth session. Usually it lasts about two sessions. If it extends much beyond this, say for four sessions, the need to re-evaluate becomes apparent. The therapy can become purely repetitious. For example, to continue indefinitely asking the couple to re-invest themselves in their relationship is unlikely to be productive. The therapist should evaluate this repetition with the couple in the light of agreed goals, as long-term repetition is seldom beneficial. Assuming that this has not happened and the couple have moved through the process so far, then phase three begins.

Before going on to phase three attention needs to be drawn to a problem which sometimes occurs during phase two. One or both partners may lose motivation and regress to the old destructive patterns of interaction. This is especially difficult to deal with if both partners lose motivation at the same time. If only one has lost motivation, the focus with the other partner is primarily on sustaining motivation while allowing the other space to re-invest. In either case, reference to the change previously achieved, even though it was only temporary, should be used as a means of enabling the reinvestment. Fundamentally, the couple should now know that they can achieve more satisfaction. The barrier to achieving this is likely to be their inability to decide to do so and not an inability to meet these needs. The objective of phase three, the consolidation phase, is to help the couple to consolidate the affectional needs-meeting-process begun in phase two. This involves bringing therapy to an end with the couple feeling sufficiently secure in their new interaction pattern to allow the unaided resolution of presenting problems.

Having been enabled in phase two to experience positive interchange through responding to affectional needs, the couple now face the task of learning to acquire and maintain this interaction without help from outside. This is done through the couple being helped to establish a pattern of interaction that maintains and enlarges positive interchange. Put in behavioural terms, sustaining conditions within the relationship have to be found to maintain the new positive responses.

Phase three of Reinvestment Therapy begins with each partner being able to respond to the efforts made by the other to effect positive change. For example, when one partner makes efforts to show understanding of the other and the other is helped to acknowledge this effort, the couple are setting up new patterns of interaction. They are giving positive feedback to each other, a feedback that will provide sustaining conditions for the new interaction pattern.

An example of this process can be seen with Connie and Geoff. Whenever Connie felt low without their being any clearly identifiable reason for it, Geoff tended to see it as being a criticism of him. He wondered why Connie could get so unhappy when he was doing his best to make her happy. As a result of this interpretation and also because of the negative way Connie sought his emotional support, Geoff tended to react defensively. He was likely to say to her something like this: "Pull yourself together, Connie; what's wrong with you now?" Connie would then criticize Geoff, and let him know how unhelpful his reply was. Defensively, he would shout back at her. She would cry and soon both would be yelling at each other. Eventually Geoff would leave in a rage and not return for several hours, which left Connie worse off than before she sought his emotional understanding.

In the exploration phase of therapy they were both able to see this negative pattern of interaction and thus able to alter it. The new pattern involved Connie being less negative in her approach to Geoff and his being less defensive in his response. In this altered interaction he was able to give understanding responses which facilitated Connie to share her concerns. The shouting and crying were eliminated. Geoff did not feel the need to escape, and Connie felt understood.

However, in spite of this apparent "happy" outcome, this changed pattern would be unlikely to continue unless Connie and Geoff could find some way of maintaining it. This is the task of the consolidation phase. In the case of Connie and Geoff this was provided by Connie being able to give positive feedback to Geoff by expressing to him her feeling of being emotionally understood. Thus the sustaining condition for this new interaction included: Connie's positive feedback to Geoff; Geoff's changed response to Connie; Connie's feeling of being emotionally supported; Geoff not feeling criticized and both of them feeling satisfaction from their new pattern of interaction. Through these changes they were finding and expanding new sources of affection in their relationship.

For the couple to be helped to interact with each other on a feeling level requires considerable risk for them initially, as it involves both being open to sharing and receiving expressions of feelings. A relationship which has produced disappointment and pain, like that of Connie and Geoff, is likely to have resulted in the couple retreating from sharing on a feeling level. They are now asked to assure each other that they will not hurt one another. Even though this assurance is sought, they need to be aware that this does not constitute a guarantee. A risk still exists but the manifestation of goodwill helps to reduce it. The process involved here is that of making conscious the positive effect they have on each other as a result of changed behaviour and becoming aware of the control each can exercise over himself/herself.[2] When they take this risk, the couple has begun to build a new, more satisfying relationship. The couple will need a lot of encouragement and support from the therapist, for in learning new behaviour they are likely to relapse into old negative patterns. Also some couples will find it more difficult than others to change. To facilitate the learning which helps a couple to consolidate the new interaction, they should be made aware of some basic principles of learning. For example, wanting to change does not usually bring about spontaneous change. New behaviour has to be learned. Also, when the therapist is monitoring new learning, the results should be measured throughout the complete time-phase, and not just the period immediately preceding the interview.

The learning in the consolidation phase is a continuous process and, like all other learning, it involves practice. The therapy session becomes primarily instructional with the time between sessions becoming periods of learning for the couple. Each therapy session, in addition to checking out tasks assigned, also involves monitoring the couple's interaction for the intervening period. Only difficulties of an interactional nature are dealt with. If they are not encountering difficulties with learning, the couple is either encouraged to maintain the level of interaction achieved, or to progress further until they feel confident in their new patterns of interaction. This level of confidence is achieved when the new behaviour becomes, as it were, its own reinforcer. In other words, the sustaining conditions become the satisfaction derived from the new interaction, just as the sustaining conditions of the old patterns were the self-protective manoeuvres mentioned earlier.

The couple should now be ready to terminate their therapy, the sessions up to now having been weekly with possibly a longer period between the last two. A number of weeks without therapy sessions before therapy ends is helpful at this time. This period enables the couple to try their new patterns of interaction unaided, while being secure in the knowledge that should something go wrong, they will be offered an opportunity of re-examining the situation.

The final session, in addition to clarifying issues involved with the new interaction, should also include discussion of the original presenting problems. Usually this discussion amounts to no more than a checking out, as the couple should now be able to resolve these difficulties unaided. If they are, therapy is terminated. If they are not, a short-term contract may need to be negotiated, extending the period of therapy, but terminating in a similar manner. The need for this extension can be either a result of difficulties with the new interaction or because of a problem that requires some additional attention.

The consolidation phase can take from two to four sessions. Depending on the couple, it is possible to have the first of these sessions overlap with the last in the exploration phase. In this case, the minimum number of sessions the total therapy process can take is four. The usual number is somewhere between six and ten sessions, depending on each couple's own unique sense of pacing.

Reinvestment Therapy is intended for use with couples experiencing unhappiness as a result of social change. It is not suitable for use with all couples. Some people may not be able to approach a search for sources of affection for the variety of reasons previously mentioned. This does not mean, of course, that they are not equally in need of affection.

There are many reasons why people have marital difficulties and any approach to marital therapy must take account of these different causes. Reinvestment Therapy is one approach. It is specifically designed for those couples whose marriages have run into difficulty because of their changing expectations of each other and of marriage.

By focusing on these changing expectations, the couple are enabled to re-define their marital conflict in these terms and within the wider context of change in society. In this way they can release themselves from a defensive blaming relationship to one in which they can reinvest and thereby find and develop more satisfying sources of affection in each other.

NOTES

1. As noted before, not all couples will achieve this fulfilment due to such factors as an inability to become involved in a close inter-personal relationship. These couples would probably require a different approach to therapy than the one presented here.

2. The word "control" is used because it emphasizes to the couple that they play a major part in determining the nature of the interaction in their own relationship. Couples frequently think that interaction in the relationship is determined by factors outside of themselves such as fate, or they believe that people cannot change. They often confuse change in behaviour with personality change.

Chapter 7

Measuring Success

Among the uncertainties facing any marital therapist is that of trying to gauge whether or not the interventions being used are indeed helping the couple to resolve their problems and develop a more satisfying marital relationship. Frequently reliance is on the couple's feedback, or when this feedback is absent, on guessing. While there are, of course, many measures to evaluate mutual satisfaction that can be used with couples during the course of therapy, not many therapists either use them or see them as conducive to the therapy process.

A further, related difficulty facing marital therapists is the absence of any established criteria against which to measure a good marriage. There is no one marriage, be it institutional, companionship, or any blend of the two along the role compatibility continuum that can act as a reference point in this regard. Each marriage relationship is not only different from all others, but also constantly in a process of change. In addition to this, the difficulty of comparison is all the greater because a relationship experienced by one person as fulfilling might be considered by another as the reverse. Differences in personalities, expectations, needs and values all go to make up the uniqueness of each relationship. Faced with these factors, it is obvious that the marital therapist who attempts to measure marital therapy progress in terms of movement of a couple towards some preconceived idea of what constitutes a good marriage is engaged in a useless exercise, or worse still, approaches couples not as a therapist, but as a judge.

In spite of these difficulties, it is of course possible for the marital therapist to keep some track of the couple's response to marital therapy. The keeping of written records that highlight the main events of each session is probably the most widely used mechanism for doing this. Record-keeping can, however, be burdensome at times, especially if time between sessions is limited. To cope with this, therapists often keep a sort of shorthand account of what has happened. While these records are an invaluable aid to the therapist, they seldom track with any degree of reliability the couple's progress through time, unless some specific criteria are used for measurement.

When objective tests are not used and/or when an independent rater is not available, the therapist tends to look for indicators which have a minimum reliance on the his or her own subjective impressions. This, then, leaves essentially two categories from which to select: those indicators which rely totally on the couple's own assessment of the marital therapy, and those which are clearly observable. Using these criteria, a number of items can be identified as helpful indicators of a couple's movement towards a resolution of their marital problems during marital therapy. The following listing of indicators represents those which emerged from the content analysis of the case records used in this study.

(a) Both partners attend for therapy

The attendance of both husband and wife at marital therapy, while not necessarily an indication of problem-solving, is, however, significant in itself. Their presence makes possible the engagement of the couple in marital therapy, which is a first step towards getting effective help. This does not mean, of course, that simply by being present the couple have begun problem-solving or, indeed, are even motivated for, or interested in, marital therapy. There are many reasons why both partners might attend that have nothing to do with the proper function of marital therapy. They may come to defend themselves, or to gain the support of the therapist in some anticipated litigation.

However, if only one partner attends, the work of the therapist is frequently directed towards the involvement of the other one. Therefore, the presence of both partners at least makes it possible to explore the couple's motives and also facilitates the engagement of both individuals in marital therapy. Thus, the attendance of both partners, something which is clearly observable, can be taken as an indicator of movement towards problem-solving.

(b) Both partners say they are willing to work on relationship.

Attendance of the couple for marital therapy is obviously not enough. Sometimes people attending for marital therapy are merely seeking changes in their spouse. This is very common insofar as people in unhappy marriages may feel that they have already done almost everything possible individually to bring about a change, and that therefore any change that comes must come, initially at least, from the other person. In addition to this, it is not uncommon for people to come expecting the therapy session to change their marriage while they continue to behave between sessions much as they had before. In cases like this, the commitment is not that the couple will work on the marriage, but that the therapist will. Clearly, this is of little help to the couple.

Therefore, an initial task for the marital therapist is frequently to try to get a commitment from each partner to work on improving the marriage. The willingness of both to do this can be taken as a further indicator of movement towards solving the problems. If the couple have given this commitment, but later withdraw it for some reason or other, such as the development of new hostilities, their recommitment should also be taken as an indicator.

(c) Each time tasks assigned are carried out

An integral part of Reinvestment Therapy is the work a couple do between sessions. Couples often need some guidelines on how to do this work. One way is to give them specific tasks to do as they arise out of the therapy sessions. Any attempt by the couple at doing these tasks—or homework as it might be called—is a strong indicator of their willingness to be engaged in solving the problems.

Success or failure in these tasks should not be confused with the couple's attempt to do them. The latter is what is of significance here. The former is often the focus of on-going marital therapy sessions in which either new tasks are assigned or blocks to achieving the initial tasks are examined.

(d) Either partner reports decrease in conflict and tension since last session
Before a couple can move towards the development of a more constructive and rewarding relationship they first need to reduce the amount of conflict and tension that exists in their present interaction. Such a reduction is not problem-solving, but it does create a climate within which problem-solving can take place. Thus, any decrease in conflict and tension since the last session, as reported by either partner, is another indicator of movement towards problem-solving. Both partners simultaneously reporting such a decrease indicates even further movement in this direction.

(e) Either partner reports increased satisfaction in relationship since last session
Increased satisfaction with the relationship does not necessarily follow from a decrease in conflict and tension. Both may be closely inter-related but they are separate processes and need to be seen as such by the reinvestment therapist. To assume that one follows from the other or is always dependent on the other can result in the therapist cutting off a significant aspect of the couple's interaction. Increased satisfaction generally requires new interaction patterns and not simply a reduction in previous negative behaviour-patterns. Thus, when either partner reports increased satisfaction, it can be taken as a further indicator of movement towards problem-solving. If the satisfaction is expressed by both partners then this is an additional

sign of movement.

It should be noted that for both items (d) and (e), a distinction is made between a partner reporting a change and both partners reporting change. This is to draw attention to different levels of change within the relationship. Obviously, a situation where only one partner experiences improvement is significantly different to a situation where both partners experience this change.

In addition, these two items might not always lead to a resolution of the couple's problems or necessarily reflect genuine movement in this direction. For example, absence of conflict might simply be avoidance of conflict or the result of disengagement from the relationship. Here the use of these factors is as indicators that are easily available to the marital therapist and which, when taken with the other indicators, help in plotting a couple's movement through Reinvestment Therapy. They are not, and the same is true for the remainder of the indicators, absolute criteria in their own right.

(f) Either partner feels understood by the other as a new experience

When either partner begins to feel that the other understands her/him and that this is either a new experience or the revival of a long-absent experience, there is a strong likelihood that the couple are further progressing towards problem-solving. The emphasis here is on the *experience* of being understood, which is quite different from attempts by either partner at understanding the other. Both partners might well consider themselves as always trying to understand the other one, but neither might feel understood. Thus, it is the experience of *feeling* understood that is taken as the indicator.

(g) Both partners supportive to each other during interview

As a couple begins to develop new and more rewarding patterns of interaction, their new behaviour with each other should be observable in the therapy sessions. One such observable change would be their ability to be supportive to each other during a session. This support, however, would need to be more than a single supportive comment or isolated intervention if it is to reflect change in interaction patterns. When support like this is maintained throughout a session it can be taken as indicating continued movement of the couple towards an enhanced relationship.

(h) Displays of non-verbal signs of improvement in interaction

Non-verbal signs such as holding hands, improved personal appearance and changes in seating arrangement can also be taken as indicators of an improvement in the relationship. The indication can be taken from either the use of several non-verbal signs together such as sitting close to one another, looking directly at each other and smiling, or from a single act such as placing arms around one another. Non-verbal signs like those described are taken as indications of improvement only the first time they appear and not for each subsequent occurrence.

(i) Couple resolve problems on their own that had previously presented difficulty
A test of a couple's improved relationship is their ability to deal unaided with difficulties that arise between them outside of therapy sessions. Couples who have only reached a level of conflict-avoidance and who have not developed new interaction patterns will, most likely, be unable to do this. The number of problems or difficulties resolved is less important than the couple's ability to resolve them. Thus, the indicator is taken from the process of problem-solving rather than the particular problem or problems solved. If the couple can maintain this problem-solving between different sessions, then each new period of problem-solving (a period being the time between any two consecutive sessions) is taken as a further indication of their continued movement towards an enhanced relationship.

(j) Couple maintain improvements for several weeks on their own or over holiday periods
Time, the proverbial healer of wounds, is also a good test of the cure. Couples who can maintain improvements during a break of several weeks between sessions are likely to have at least begun the consolidation of positive ways of interaction. This is also true if they can maintain improvements over holiday periods such as Christmas. The reason for this is that expectations are usually high for holiday periods, and if little progress has been made in the development of new interaction patterns, the expectations are likely to lead to disappointment.

(k) Couple's presenting problems resolved

The final indicator used in plotting a couple's progression towards a more satisfying relationship is the resolution of the problems the couple first presented when seeking help. These are referred to as "presenting problems" because they might not have been the direct focus of therapy for a variety of reasons. For example, they could have been so global in their presentation as to render them unmanageable: for example, poor communication or emotional distance. These problems are encountered by most people with relationship difficulties.

It is the disappearance of these problems and not how they were resolved that is taken as the indicator. Sometimes they may need special attention and sometimes they simply cease to exist when other aspects of the relationship change. Sexual problems are a good example of both of these, i.e. sometimes couples need specific help in dealing with sexual problems; at other times these problems resolve themselves when a couple succeed in developing other aspects of their relationship.

By noting these factors, or similar factors, a marital therapist can keep some track of a couple's progress through marital therapy. They are not absolute criteria in their own right, but serve as helpful indicators of a couple's movement towards problem-solving in an enhanced relationship. As indicators they simply point a way or mark an intended course.

An analogy can be drawn with an indicator on a car. For example, a blinking amber light on the left side of the car may be a signal that the driver intends to turn left. However, it could also mean that the driver forgot to turn it off after the last left turn, is undecided what direction to turn next, or indeed that the car has a mechanical fault. Whatever the possible meaning, we all tend to pay attention to the indication even if only to see what in fact it does mean. The indicators offered here are intended as having much the same function; they are visible signs of a possible movement in one direction.

A chart of these indicators can be constructed as in Diagram 5 (p. 86) for easy use and reference by the marital therapist. They are given in a progressive form with those more likely to occur at the start of therapy listed at the beginning. The progression of indicators on the chart also roughly coincides with the three phases in the approach to Reinvestment Therapy previously described. Items (a), (b), (c) and (d) correspond to the engagement phase. Items (e), (f), (g) and (h) occur primarily during the exploration phase, and items (i), (j) and (k) are more likely to be present in the consolidation phase. Item (c), although listed here as occurring during the engagement phase, in fact runs all through the Reinvestment Therapy process. Its first occurrence, however, is normally during the engagement phase, and it can frequently act as a test of the couple's commitment to changing their relationship.

DIAGRAM 5:   MARITAL THERAPY INDICATORS

ENGAGEMENT PHASE

(a) Both partners attend marital therapy

(b) When both partners say for the first time that they are willing to work on the marriage, and if there has been a relapse period involving withdrawal from marital therapy for either partner, then when they say it again.

(c) Each time tasks assigned are carried out.

(d) Either partner reports decrease in conflict and tension since the last session.

EXPLORATION PHASE

(e) Either partner reports increased satisfaction in their relationship since the last session.

(f) Either partner feels understood by the other as a new experience.

(g) Both partners supportive to each other during interview.

(h) Displays of non-verbal signs of improvement in the couple's interaction.

CONSOLIDATION PHASE

(i) Couple resolve problems on their own that had previously presented difficulty.

(j) Couple maintain improvements for several weeks on their own or over holiday periods.

(k) Couple's presenting problems resolved.

By assigning a numerical value of one to each of these indicators, it is possible to represent a couple's progress through marital therapy on a graph. Assigning the same value to each indicator is purely arbitrary, but it does avoid placing them in a ranking order. While this could lead to a distorted representation of the couple's progress it does take account of the varied difficulty each item could represent to different couples. For example, attendance by both partners, indicator (a) on the chart, could have much less significance for one couple than for another, just as committing oneself to working on the marriage, indicator (b) on the chart, might, and so on.

The purpose of the graph is to provide the reinvestment therapist with an easy-to-use visual representation of the couple's general direction in Reinvestment Therapy. By using the small letter (a), (b), etc., from the chart on Diagram 5 where the points have been plotted on the graph, the reasons for the direction become quite apparent. Progress is measured in units of one along the vertical axis as illustrated in Diagram 6 (p. 88).

DIAGRAM 6.   GRAPH SHOWING A COUPLE'S
PROGRESS THROUGH MARITAL THERAPY

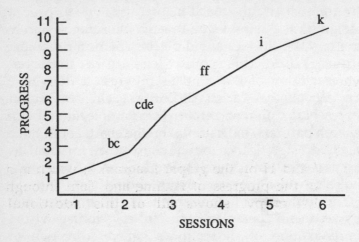

As can be seen in Diagram 6, both partners attended
for the first session (a). By the second they had both
committed themselves to working on the relationship
(b) and attempted the task assigned in the first session
(c). Further progress can be seen in the third session
where assigned task was again attempted (c) and one
of the partners reported a decrease in conflict (d) and
an increase in satisfaction (e). In the fourth session both
partners reported feeling understood by the other (f,),
and by the fifth session they had resolved problems on
their own (i). In the sixth and final session they
reported that the presenting problems were resolved
(k).

In addition to the couple's progress through therapy
as represented by the marital therapy indicators in
Diagram 4, it is possible to show other variables on the

graph. First of all, it would be more helpful to be able to see the time sequence of sessions rather than merely the number of sessions. This can easily be done by dividing the horizontal axis into time periods such as weeks. Also, the type of interviews can be represented on the graph by using the capital letter J, H and W, where J represents a joint interview, H represents a session where the husband only was present, and W represents a session where only the woman was present. If both persons were seen on the same day, but in separate interviews, this can be shown by writing both W and H on the graph. Diagram 7, which is a graph of the progress of Pauline and Tom through marital therapy, shows all of this additional information

DIAGRAM 7:   GRAPH SHOWING A COUPLE'S
PROGRESS OVER TIME IN MARITAL THERAPY

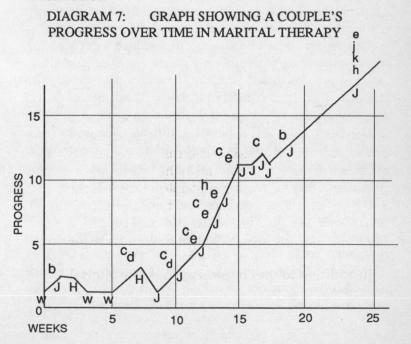

Using the letter codes from Diagram 5 and the code on the graph itself, Diagram 7 is largely self-explanatory. The apparent lack of progress in the beginning of therapy was related to lack of investment on the part of both Pauline and Tom to change in the marriage. They attended but had no expectation that their relationship would become more satisfying. When they were helped to work through these feelings and invest themselves in marital therapy, progress was relatively rapid.

Pauline had a history of reactive depression with suicidal attempts followed by periods of hospitalization, and was referred for marital therapy within the clinic itself. The poor marriage relationship had been identified as a contributing factor to her depression. There was also a parent-child relationship difficulty. Tom tended to see the difficulties in this relationship as a consequence of Pauline's depression. He was helped to focus on the marriage relationship. Tom had excluded Pauline emotionally from the family. This had contributed to her feelings of being overwhelmed by emotional problems such as lack of self-esteem and belief in her ability to change herself, feelings of failure as a parent and fear of pregnancy. This last fear also produced guilt feelings as she was not responding to Tom's sexual expectations. By reinvesting himself in a relationship with his wife on an emotional level, during the period of marital therapy, Tom helped to relieve many of the pressures for her. Both were then able to work together on improving their relationship and began to experience satisfaction from one another. When the couple were able to maintain and further improve their relationship on their own after week twenty four, the case was terminated.

Looking at the graph on Diagram 7, the first trough is explained by Pauline's feelings of hopelessness about the marriage which led her to say that she was thinking about separation and was therefore unable to commit herself to working on the relationship. The second trough was due to Tom's withdrawal of commitment to work on the marriage and Pauline doing the same. This followed an unsatisfactory attempt at sexual intercourse. The slight dip towards the end occurred when Pauline, through fear of being hurt by Tom, pulled back again on her commitment to work on the marriage. Her susequent re-commitment (b) and Tom's response resulted in both reporting increased satisfaction (e), and success in maintaining improvements over a period of time (j) leading to a resolution of presenting problems (k). In the final interview they smiled at each other and were able to reach out and touch one another (h).

The use of marital therapy indicators, either on their own or for illustrative purposes, like the graphic representation of a couple's progress through Reinvestment Therapy, can provide the therapist with useful material, irrespective of the approach being used. The indicators listed above were developed as a result of a content analysis of the case records of couples seeking marital therapy when the approach used was Reinvestment Therapy. However, all of the items could also apply with the use of other approaches—for example, a psychodynamic approach to marital therapy—assuming the objectives of marital therapy are the same. It is the cause of unhappiness that differs and that therefore requires different remedies, not the anticipated outcomes.

Finally, reference to indicators such as those already described draw attention to goals and the means of achieving them at any particular time during Reinvestment Therapy. There are always goals within goals and goals beside goals and goals that are means to other goals and means that are goals themselves. In other words, there are many streams of goals operating at any one time. These marital therapy indicators help in identifying one such stream, i.e. those that deal with the couple's movement towards an enhanced relationship. For example, a couple need to be engaged in marital therapy before they can use it, and as such their engagement is an implicit goal. When both partners are committed to changing the marriage, one of the indicators used above, it can be assumed that this goal is being achieved. In the next chapter, another stream of goals is identified, that is, intermediate goals of marital therapy.

Chapter 8

Goal Setting

The factors making for good or bad relationships are in some ways as varied as the people involved. However, some factors which facilitate couples in having a more fulfilling relationship emerged out of the content analysis of the case records of couples in this study. Not solutions in themselves, they are objectives or goals which, when achieved, make it more likely that the couple will resolve their problem. They are presented here as goals for marital therapy but they can be used by all couples the better to understand their own relationship.

At any given time during the process of marital therapy the therapist is concerned with the achievement of particular goals. These goals may or may not be shared by the couple. In fact, not all goals can be agreed. For example, a couple seeking marital therapy but lacking in motivation are unlikely to ask a marital therapist to motivate them. The therapist usually establishes this type of goal. It is with these goals that this chapter is concerned; that is, goals that the marital therapist is trying to achieve, whether or not the couple are involved in their selection. As such, these goals are quite distinct from those that are selected by the couple and then mutually agreed with the therapist.

All helping relationships contain numerous elements of intervention, even the most non-directive psychotherapies. The helping person is constantly sending messages whether intentionally or not. Smiling, frowning, remaining silent, talking; all send signals that affect interaction with the therapist. The degree of their effect may differ, but they are all intervening processes, or parts thereof. The intervening process can be specific or non-specific, overt or covert. If the process affects the couple's functioning, whether intended to or not, it is an intervention. Likewise, a process which is intended to affect the couple's function, whether it does so or not, is also an intervention.

All such interventions have two features. These consist of the process of intervention itself, and the goal of the intervention. The process basically refers to the form or type of the intervention. For example, it could be the giving of support, information or advice. The goal, on the other hand, is intended result of the intervention used. Take, for example, a person who decides to stay in the relationship as a result of support given by the therapist during a particularly difficult time. In this case, the process or form of intervention used is the giving of support by the therapist while the goal of the intervention is the person remaining in the relationship.

In this chapter, the concern is not with the form of intervention, but with the actual goal of the intervention. Thus, the focus is on what the marital therapist is trying to achieve with a couple at any particular time during their involvement in marital therapy and not the interventions used to achieve these goals. The concern is with what the therapist is trying to achieve rather than how it is achieved. The reason for emphasising the goal is because different therapists use different means for achieving the same goals just as different types of interventions can be used by the same therapist for the achievement of the same goal.

At any particular time in the therapy process, the therapist will be working with the couple on achieving short-term, intermediate and long-term goals. These three can overlap or be quite distinct. The long-term goals are the more global generalized goals of the therapy, such as promoting greater satisfaction in the relationship. Short-term goals are more immediate and generally relate to the achievement of either the long-term or intermediate goals. These need not always be explicit. During any single therapy session there could be numerous short-term, explicit and implicit goals. This is illustrated in the following sequence: a couple are helped to relate (short-term goal one), to enable them to begin sharing feelings of disappointment (short-term goal two), so that they can hear what the other person has to say (short-term goal three) and so on.

Intermediate goals are more explicit, extend over a longer period of therapy and their achievement is necessary to the attainment of long-term goals. This chapter is concerned with these intermediate goals. In determining what constitutes an intermediate goal, specific criteria are used. An intermediate goal is one which (1) is the major goal of the intervention for one or more interviews; (2) is used by the therapist as a goal of his/her choice, that is, one about which the therapist is explicit; and (3) enables the couple, or one of the partners in achieving it to move to a further stage in the marital therapy process.

Using these criteria a content analysis of cases of couples seeking marital therapy revealed twelve intermediate goals. These intermediate goals can be divided into two main types: those that deal primarily with the promotion of motivation and those that are concerned with effecting change in the interaction between the partners. Although motivation and change are closely related and at times may even appear inseparable, the distinction is based on the intention of the intervention.

For example, if the intention of a particular intervention is to motivate one of the partners to continue working on the relationship, then it is classified as a motivation intervention. If, on the other hand, the intention of the intervention is to facilitate interactional change such as improving communication on a feeling level, then it is classified as a change goal. On the basis of this distinction, intermediate goals can be classified as being predominantly either motivational or change goals. The first of these types focuses on the individual while the second focuses on interactional patterns. Thus the two sets of goals are also on two different levels. Motivational goals are on an individual level while change goals are on a systemic level.

An intermediate motivational goal is any intermediate goal of the marital therapist that has, as its primary intention, the promotion of motivation on the part of either partner in the relationship. In this study the following six motivational goals emerged from the content analysis as being of particular importance: (i) either or both partners deciding to work on the relationship; (ii) accepting the need to change self; (iii) being able to see the part played by self in the conflict; (iv) being willing to take risks in the relationship; (v) trusting the other partner in the relationship; and (vi) maintaining personal investment in the relationship.

(i) Either or both partners deciding to work on the relationship

Most couples seeking marital therapy require some help with motivation to work on the relationship because of the very nature of their situation. Sometimes this may only require clarification of motives, distance from a recent destructive event, seeing the relationship from a different perspective, or some other similar help that does not require intensive work on the part of the therapist as already indicated. Willingness to attend for marital therapy even with the expressed desire to work on the relationship is not by itself an indication of motivation. The couple might seek help with their relationship for many reasons— such as following through a referral or because of their attitudes to separation—that have nothing to do with the individual's desire to have a mutually fulfilling relationship with the other person per se.

Using the fact of either or both partners deciding to work on the relationship as a goal of intervention occurs when the lack of commitment to working on the relationship by one or both partners is identified as a major block to changing the relationship. This lack of commitment can be manifested by resistance either in the initial stages of the marital therapy, or as a recurring obstacle at later stages.

Apart from the more obvious manifestations of resistance, such as one partner failing to attend for interviews, resistance to working on the relationship can be difficult to identify in the initial stages of therapy. Less obvious resistance and lack of motivation are seen in situations where, for example, one partner has difficulty agreeing to work on the relationship for its own sake, or seeks to lay down conditions for the other partner before agreeing. In the on-going marital therapy process lack of commitment is often reflected in the failure to carry out agreed tasks between therapy sessions.

The establishment of a commitment to work on the relationship as a goal of intervention is illustrated by the case of Joan and Michael. Before the therapist saw them both together, Joan had attended on her own with the expressed desire of improving their relationship. Her husband was overseas at the time and only home on occasional weekends. Since the individual sessions did not appear to be affecting any change in the relationship, it was agreed to postpone marital therapy until both could attend. Several months later marital therapy recommenced. However, no change was reported until the fourth interview of the second period of therapy. The goal of intervention with Joan up to that time had been in trying to motivate her to work on the relationship, something she had not being doing even though she had willingly attended for therapy. Her attendance for individual sessions when her husband was unable to attend was not, as might be assumed, an indication of her motivation to work on the relationship. Instead, her lack of motivation was manifested in her desire to lay down conditions, such as having Michael agree to leaving the family home if they separated after therapy. Joan felt that her conditions were reasonable and she had no awareness of the obstacle these conditions represented to an open commitment to working on the relationship for its own sake. Helping her to work through these feelings was the major goal of intervention in the early stages of the marital therapy and it was not until she could accept an unconditional commitment that any progress was made.

(ii) Accepting the need to change oneself

Closely associated with the preceding goal of intervention is the goal of accepting the need to change oneself. An individual or couple may be committed to working on the relationship, but this does not necessarily mean that they are willing to change themselves. For example, one or both partners may place all the responsibility for change on the other, or see the relationship as something abstract and apart from themselves.

Reinvestment Therapy contains an implicit expectation of personal change in attitudes, feelings and behaviour. It is not always necessary to make this explicit, as some couples readily see the necessity for this change. With others, the mere process of making it explicit in a supportive, educative manner suffices. However, if simple techniques such as those just described do not bring a commitment to changing the self, it becomes necessary to make this a major focus of intervention and as such an intermediate motivational goal. Thus, it becomes a specific task of the therapy process. As a goal, it is used when either partner is expecting and/or wants the relationship to change, but is not willing, or is unaware of the need to effect personal change as a prerequisite for change in the relationship. This arises in situations where either a partner sees no need for change, or feels that prior to this he/she tried everything, or when the solution is thought to consist of effecting change in the other person.

Nicholas and Carmel both seemed keen to work on improving their relationship. Nicholas in particular seemed highly motivated. He said that he was prepared to do anything, as it were, to bring about a happy relationship between himself and Carmel. The one major block to achieving this was, he felt, Carmel's rejection of his sexual overtures. He saw himself as a caring, sensitive partner who was as concerned about Carmel's sexual needs as he was about his own. Within this perception of the relationship, however, he was unable to see what changes he could make other than being ready to respond to changes in Carmel. While she did not see Nicholas quite as he saw himself, Carmel did think of him as being generally a good partner and she too was inclined to focus on her lack of sexual response as the major obstacle to a better relationship.

On further exploration it emerged that Carmel and Nicholas had a satisfactory sexual relationship up to about two years ago, but that Carmel had begun to feel distant from Nicholas for some time before that. She somehow felt inadequate in relation to him and thought that she could not measure up to his expectations in many ways, one of which was in their sexual relationship. Underlying this was a feeling that Nicholas was constantly pushing her to change, and this had led to her fear that he really did not accept her as she was. Before Carmel and Nicholas could begin a resolution of their difficulties, Nicholas had to see that he needed to change too, and not just be ready to respond to Carmel's changes. His very expectation of change in Carmel was itself a major obstacle to changing the relationship. Nicholas's attitude could have been summed up as "I am ready to do anything for this relationship except change myself."

A couple who attempt to change their relationship without changing themselves in some way are attempting the impossible, and if the expectation is to change the other person, as was the case with Nicholas, then the means by which they hope to improve the relationship becomes the very antithesis of what constitutes a mutually satisfying relationship—that is rejection. A basic ingredient of a fulfilling relationship is acceptance. Because of the constant pressure to change, Carmel certainly did not feel accepted by Nicholas.

(iii) Being able to see the part played by oneself in conflict

In the context of marital conflict, partners often fail to see the part they play in the conflict, attributing the difficulties either to the other person or to some force outside themselves. Being helped to see one's own part in the conflict and its consequent resolution frequently becomes an intermediate goal of intervention. This is a motivational goal because the couple cannot move towards the resolution of their problems without accepting that they have a part to play in bringing this resolution about. (This is closely associated with the previous goal of accepting the need to change oneself.)

The goal of this intervention is similar to the development of insight. The difference is that here the goal is exclusively concerned with having each partner accept his/her part in the conflict. It has to do with each being able to accept that the relationship is an interaction of which they are both a part, and over which they can individually exercise some influence. For as long as one of the partners maintains that the change must come from the other person, or other sources outside of themselves, then they must also feel out of control of the relationship.

Some couples may be highly motivated to work on their relationship and willing to change themselves in the process, but simply may not have an awareness of the effect they have on each other. Enabling them to develop this awareness can often be a relatively simple but necessary process. When there is resistance to accepting this responsibility, or where a person has very little insight into his/her own behavior, the process becomes a major intervention, and as such its achievement becomes an intermediate motivational goal of the therapy.

Mary and Richard provide a good example of this inability to see their own part in the conflict. Both requested therapy and both were willing to change in order to achieve a resolution of their conflict.

However, Richard was unable to see his part in the conflict. Mary had been involved emotionally with another man. While Mary still felt attached to this man, she had discontinued meeting him and now wanted to reinvest herself with her partner. Richard was open to this and very much wanted a relationship with Mary, but was unable to see his part in the conflict. For him, the problem centered around Mary's affair. Richard could not see what he could do to build a relationship with Mary now.

Because he had been very hurt by Mary's other relationship, Richard's attitude now bordered on "righteous indignation," as a defence against the feeling of rejection. He could only see his relationship with her as highly successful up to the time of the other involvement, a view not shared by Mary. For Richard to see his part in the conflict became an intermediate goal because he could not move beyond this point until he could see it. He did succeed and was able to move on with Mary towards resolving their conflict together. Many people, however, are unable to take such a step and remain stuck at this point.

(iv) Being willing to take risks in the relationship
All relationships involve some risk. These risks include the possibility of rejection, feelings of vulnerability, appearing dependent and so on. People are not always conscious of the risks involved in certain relationships. When they are, they sometimes decide to take the risks and become involved in the relationship anyway. Other people try to avoid these risks by avoiding relationships. Extreme forms of risk

avoidance are usually symptomatic of some underlying personality difficulty.

There are also risks involved in a marriage relationship. Apart from the intensity of the relationship, the risks are no different from those in any other relationship. Couples seeking therapy have usually decreased their risk-taking in the relationship because the risks have proved too great. In therapy the couple are expected to reinvest themselves in a relationship which is currently producing great pain. Some couples come for therapy prepared to take the risk. Others are not prepared and need help to enable them to take this risk. It is in this situation that helping a couple or individual partner to take the risk of reinvestment becomes an intermediate motivational goal.

Risk-taking was particularly difficult for Harry in his relationship with Brenda. He wanted to improve the relationship, was willing to change himself and could even see his part in the conflicts, but could not bring himself to tell her the extent of his financial debts. He felt that she would use this information against him in subsequent arguments. He was also unable to share with her his feelings of hurt and vulnerability as he thought this might be interpreted by her as weakness. Harry wanted a guarantee, as it were, that if he shared these matters with Brenda, she would not misuse them. Her promises did not seem sufficient to him; he wanted to be sure. The only way Harry could get over this difficulty of sharing with Brenda was to take the risk involved in the sharing. He was not able to do this on his own.

The difficulty in taking risks, although usually

related to the hurt experienced in the relationship, can also have other origins. This is frequently found where one partner has a generalized difficulty in risking him/herself in relationships either as a result of past negative experiences, or the absence of any close relationship in his/her past life. Unless both partners are willing to take risks in their own relationship, they cannot be helped to meet each other's affectional needs. Without the risks, they would have to settle for a resolution of their conflicts which does not include emotional intimacy.

(v) Trusting the other partner in the relationship
The goal of trying to get one partner to trust the other is similar to the goal of risk-taking. In fact, it is really a particular aspect of risk-taking. It is identified here as a separate intermediate motivational goal because the need for its achievement is quite distinct from the individual's willingness to risk reinvestment in the relationship.

It is an intermediate goal when either partner has difficulty trusting the other and when this difficulty prevents growth in the relationship. This is usually a result of one partner feeling that the trust he/she invested in the other person resulted in considerable pain. Illustrations of this include situations where one partner had an extra-marital involvement, grossly mishandled finances, or failed to keep confidences. In these situations the other partner's trust is often withheld until trustworthiness can be demonstrated. The resultant block to growth in the relationship is manifested in such ways as being unable to share information or to accept at face value what the other person says.

The above is illustrated by the following example of Betty and John. Betty had had an extra-marital relationship. As a result of this, John felt unable to trust her. During the time of the therapy she committed herself to discontinuing her second relationship. It then became essential that John accepted what she said at face value if any progress was to be made in the relationship. There was no way she could prove to him that she had discontinued the other relationship and for as long as he refused to trust her, the relationship between Betty and John remained grossly unequal. John's difficulty in giving Betty his trust, then, became a focus of therapy. In this situation, helping him to trust Betty became an intermediate motivational goal.

(vi) Maintaining personal investment in relationship
A recurring intermediate motivational goal in therapy is that of helping either partner or both partners to maintain their investment in the relationship. As a goal of intervention, it is somewhat similar to the giving of support, which is usually the form the intervention takes. Its purpose is quite distinct, however, from the generalized giving of support which is an integral and ongoing part of the therapy.

As a goal of intervention it has two primary uses. The first is to help one partner to maintain investment in the relationship, while the other is working through a personal difficulty that is preventing him/her from further investment in the relationship at the time. This is closely associated with movement and the different pace at which each person moves. The partner who is moving at a faster pace might give up when he/she does not feel a response from the other roughly equal to his/her own effort.

This can arise in many situations as, for example, with the case of Betty and John just cited. While John was working on his difficulty in trusting Betty, she needed help in continuing her efforts at reinvestment in the relationship with John. She found this quite hard to do as she felt that John was doing nothing to change and that all the responsibility was left with her. Thus, with her, an intermediate motivational goal was that of helping her to continue her efforts even though there seemed to her to be none on the part of John. He was in fact trying, but his pace was slower than Betty's. Taking account of people's different pace in therapy is a constant (or ongoing) problem for marital therapists.

The second use of this intermediate motivational goal is to help the couple to maintain improvements achieved in their relationship at a time during the therapy when they are at risk of losing them. This situation occurs when the couple have effected some changes but are not ready or able to move further at the time. An example of this is a couple who are prevented from making further changes after a decrease in conflict because of fear that they might not be successful. The goal of intervention in this example is to help them to maintain the decrease in conflict over a period of time until they feel more secure in their new ways of interacting. The goal is not to bring about change at this time, but, by maintaining change already achieved, to facilitate motivation for future change.

All the goals described so far are what have been called intermediate motivational goals. The emphasis on motivation is important. Change in a relationship will not take place unless the partners in the relationship are motivated to change. The need to help them with this motivation can easily be overlooked by the marital therapist.

The second type of intermediate goals are change goals. These consist of any intermediate goal of the marital therapist that has as its primary intention a change in the interaction between the partners in the relationship. The content analysis of the case studies revealed the following six intermediate change goals: (i) communicating with the partner on a feeling level; (ii) accepting the partner's feelings; (iii) performance of joint tasks; (iv) conversion of vicious circles into positive circles; (v) facilitating the resolution of specific subsidiary problems; and (vi) enhancement of self-esteem.

Agreement on the selection of intermediate motivational goals was seldom sought with the couple, but change goals always have this agreement. Their achievement depends on it. However, as identified already, the change goals under discussion here are selected by the therapist and not by the couple.

(i) Communicating with partner on a feeling level
Couples experiencing marital dissatisfaction are unlikely to have a communication network which includes the sharing of positive feelings. Their communications are more likely to include judgments about each other, whether these be in the form of

criticisms, expressions of anger and disappointment, or attempts to eliminate verbal communications entirely.

When couples are introduced to the idea of communicating with each other on a feeling level, some people will respond readily while others will need considerable help to do so. Some couples need not only encouragement to communicate on a feeling level, but actual coaching in how to do so, as it is a new element in their marital communication network. It is in these situations that helping a couple or partner in the relationship to communicate on a feeling level becomes an intermediate change goal.

Joe and Margaret had never shared feelings with each other. They both said that they would like to do so, but simply felt that they did not know how. They both had academic backgrounds and tended to relate to each other in somewhat intellectual terms. Both certainly experienced feelings and were often frustrated by the intellectual response received when attempts were made at sharing them. This frustration was the root of much of their conflict.

Joe and Margaret's intellectual interaction was largely a defence against their difficulty in communicating feelings. Since they were highly motivated they were able to learn new ways of interacting which included successful communication on a feeling level.

The goal with Joe and Margaret was to develop ways for them to share feelings with each other. This involved verbalizing feelings and, when possible, describing them in depth. Instead of simply saying that they felt—for example—*sad*, they were

encouraged to elaborate on what this meant to them
individually. For Joe, the feeling was accompanied by
a feeling of emptiness and a physical sensation like a
hollow in his abdomen. Margaret's experience of
sadness was somewhat different. For her it included
feeling alone and a desire to be held. Joe and Margaret
found it difficult to describe emotions like this at first
and often felt uncomfortable when trying. The effect of
such efforts, however, was to bring them to the
awareness that they both experienced feelings and
that these experiences were legitimate. When they
were able to elaborate on their descriptions of their
feelings (and not all couples can), it brought out very
clearly the different ways they each experienced what
they previously identified as the same emotion.
Sharing the feeling and not just the word, facilitated
their emotional closeness.

(ii) Accepting partner's feelings

The intermediate change goal of accepting the feelings
of one's partner in the relationship is closely linked to
the goal of communicating on a feeling level. They are
identified as two distinct goals because the
achievement of one does not necessarily bring about
the other. Being able to share feelings in a relationship
does not always mean that the feelings of the other
person are accepted. A crucial aspect in accepting the
feelings of another person, especially in a relationship,
is being able to distinguish between judgments about
the other person and emotional reactions to that
person. Feelings are never judgments about the other
person. They are always descriptions about the person
sharing the feeling. Once this is understood, accepting

the feelings of the partner becomes possible.

The difficulty of distinguishing between emotional responses and judgments was a source of considerable unhappiness for Susan and Andrew. They had no difficulty accepting each other's feelings when they were happy and warm ones, but if Susan should feel low, as, for instance when she felt lonely, Andrew's reactions were quite different. He interpreted the lonely feelings as a criticism of him and thus saw them as a judgment about his adequacy as a companion. For Susan, however, these feelings of loneliness were generally associated with other factors in her life such as missing her family of origin and being alone with young children most of the day.

Andrew's usual reaction to Susan was defensive and resulted in him either to trying to cheer her up or avoiding her. He would do anything to change her feelings *except* allow her to express them. Her loneliness was seen as a judgment on him which had to be changed. In fact, the feeling was a natural reaction on Susan's part to realities in her life that required nothing more than for Andrew to accept it as such. Andrew's rejection of the feeling was a rejection of part of her life, and consequently deprived her of the legitimacy not only of its expression, but also of its experience.

A second aspect of accepting the feelings of another person, as seen with the case of Susan and Andrew, is that of refraining from trying to change the feelings expressed. Many people, like Andrew, seem to find this very difficult. Efforts to change the feelings expressed nearly always contain a rejection of the feelings even if the motives are altruistic. The partner who tries to change the other's feelings is in effect saying, "I do not like the feeling you express; you feel that way because of me; or, it is my responsibility to change it." Some, like Andrew, even judge their performance as a spouse by their ability to change their partner's negative feelings. All of these responses to the feelings of the other person are simply rejections of those feelings. As such they constitute a pressure both on the person experiencing the feeling and on the person to whom the feeling is expressed. As a result both partners feel pressurized by the other to change.

(iii) Performance of joint tasks

The involvement of both partners in the performance of the same tasks, such as the management of the finances or the control of children, is an intermediate goal that is often relatively easy to achieve and brings many benefits to the couple. However, any attempt to achieve this must be related to the couple's concept of relationship. For example, a couple who do not believe in sharing these tasks cannot be engaged with the goal. They need first to subscribe to the notion that some aspects of their life can be shared.

Alan and Sally had been making good progress towards resolving their marital difficulties. However, they both felt that so long as they did their separate tasks all would go well. To some extent they felt that they were avoiding difficult areas and feared that a joint effort would lead to a return of old negative ways of interacting. The test of this was the performance of a joint task which required the co-operation of both under relatively safe conditions. This was done by agreeing on ground rules for its management should the task lead to conflict. Sally and Alan set about the task, and with the protection of the agreed conditions, they were able to complete it successfully. This gave them the courage and confidence to continue their progress towards resolving their marital difficulties.

The primary benefit derived from the performance of the joint tasks in the context of therapy is the couple's experience of working constructively with each other and the shared feelings of accomplishment when the task has been achieved. This experience is often crucial for couples who as a result of their marital dissatisfaction have experienced pain and frustration in previous efforts to work together and who are prevented by these experiences from trying to develop mutual satisfactions. Being able to perform the joint tasks successfully, as Sally and Alan did, gives a couple the confidence and encouragement to work towards the achievement of mutual satisfaction.

The couple should be involved in selecting the joint tasks. Normally a task would be something about which they have expressed some concern and that they feel would improve their own situation. A joint task selected by the marital therapist alone, like any other tasks assigned as a part of the therapy, would be of little if any use without the involvement of the couple. The important element in the performance of joint tasks is the significance attached to the task by the couple.

(iv) Conversion of vicious circles into positive circles
A vicious circle is the process whereby one negative behaviour causes a second such or a series of negative behaviours which then become the cause of the first

behaviour recurring. As referred to here in the context of relationship vicious circles are situations where the negative behaviour of one partner is a contributor to the other's negative behaviour in a circular fashion as just described. Couples are seldom aware of the existence of these vicious circles and even when they are, they are usually unable to break them.

An example of a vicious circle in relationship is illustrated by the following case extract. In a joint interview with Nancy and Patrick, the following process was observed: Patrick tried to talk to Nancy. Each time he started she interrupted him. When he stopped trying, she accused him of not saying anything and of leaving all of the talking in the interview to her. He responded with verbal abuse, which caused her to cry. He then said with great anger that all she did was cry when he tried to talk to her and then he stopped talking further to her. After a short silence, Nancy looked to the marital therapist saying, "See, he won't talk to me." Soon, the whole process started over again and a negative circle was complete, with the end of the process becoming its beginning.

(v) Facilitating resolution of specific subsidiary problems

Couples seeking therapy frequently come asking for help in resolving specific problems. Often these problems are symptomatic of the marital difficulty and attempts to resolve them are in vain. Some subsidiary problems are not symptomatic and require special attention. These are problems that are likely to continue even if the major areas of marital dissatisfaction are resolved. In these situations the resolution of specific subsidiary problems becomes an intermediate change goal.

An illustration of a subsidary problem is provided by the difficulties surrounding Jean and Steven's sexual relationship. They had come for therapy because of a number of difficulties in their relationship, most of which had been resolved after the first session. In discussing their sexual relationship they felt that it had returned to a level of satisfaction similar to when they were first married. Essentially this consisted of a somewhat mechanical approach in which Stephen reached orgasm, but Jean seldom did. Neither saw this as a contributory factor to the marital problems, but both felt that they would like a more satisfying sexual relationship. Their unsatisfactory sexual relationship was then taken up as a subsidiary problem.

The key to the solution was found in Jean's negative attitude towards sex which was largely a result of her early socialising. She felt guilty about foreplay and tended therefore either to avoid it or to feel tense if she did participate. These feelings of guilt and tension inhibited her full involvement in intercourse and consequently she seldom reached orgasm. By realising on an intellectual level, initially, that her attitudes were the source of her difficulty, she was eventually able to modify them and to translate these changes onto a feeling level. These changed feelings made possible her fuller participation in sexual relations and more mutually satisfying sexual relations for them both.

Problems like that of Steven and Jean are called subsidiary because they are not part of the main marital difficulty, but constitute problems in their own right whose resolution is not always necessary for the couple to achieve an improvement in their relationship. They are dealt with when they appear to be obstacles to progress or when the couple or individual concerned seem able to work towards their resolution. It is important to note here that not all problems should automatically be assumed by the therapist as needing solution. Some people are content once a subsidiary problem has been identified to leave it and deal with it by avoiding as much as possible the situations that bring it into focus. Others will want help in resolving the subsidiary problems and it is here that their resolution becomes a change goal.

(vi) Enhancement of self-esteem

A normal benefit resulting from improved marital relations is increased self-esteem. This results simply from the new esteem in which each partner is held by the other. However, sometimes the enhancement of self-esteem as an intermediate change goal is necessary. Marital confict by its nature can be most destructive to a person's self-esteem. Because of this the therapist may need to work towards the specific enhancement of self-esteem as in the case of the couple in the following example.

Monica and Robert had a pattern of blaming each other whenever the slightest misunderstanding arose between them. Both had felt that their self-esteem had taken quite a battering as a result of this constant blaming. Robert felt lacking in self-confidence as he considered Monica to be the stronger of the two, and he felt that he depended more on her than she did on him. Because of this he felt a constant loser in their conflicts. He dealt with this loss of confidence by being aggressive and occasionally hit Monica in anger. These acts of his further undermined his self-esteem. Monica's self-esteem was also very low. Robert's physical violence towards her, even though it was not a frequent occurrence, when coupled with his swearing and name-calling, left her feeling worthless, too.

Monica and Robert resolved most of their conflicts and began experiencing a more rewarding and constructive relationship. Both, however, needed specific help in building back their self-esteem and this became an intermediate change goal. This goal was achieved by involving them both in giving a lot of emotional support and confirmation to each other in addition to helping them to widen the base for their self-esteem to include other successful aspects of their lives.

These change goals are in some ways the crux of Reinvestment Therapy. They represent the type of change any couple will need to make if they are to maintain a mutually fulfilling relationship.

By examining the intermediate goals that the marital therapist is trying to achieve with the couple at any given time, valuable information can be gained on the couple's commitment to seeking changes in their relationship. If the intermediate goals are mainly motivational, then the therapist needs to re-examine the contract with the couple. A couple requiring this amount of motivating may need therapy, but not necessarily marital therapy. If they say that they want marital therpy, but the therapist finds all energies being used in trying to achieve motivational goals, then it is likely that the therapist is trying to achieve inappropriate goals and should, therefore, re-evaluate them with the couple. This re-evaluation can lead to termination, either as a result of the couple's decision to do so or, as is sometimes appropriate, by the therapist's decision. Change will not be achieved in the relationship if there is no commitment on the part of the couple to achieving it.

Finally, before a couple can achieve the intermediate change goals, they must first have the levels of motivation required for the motivational goals. It is not necessary to have as an intermediate goal all or even any of the motivational goals. What is significant is that the couple must have the level of motivation that would make their achievement possible.

Chapter 9

Reinvestment Therapy—a Short-Term Treatment

Reinvestment Therapy is essentially a short-term treatment approach for use in working with couples who have problems in their relationship. The short-term nature of the approach is of crucial importance for many reasons. In addition to the benefits of using a short-term approach discussed in this chapter, it is also important that couples requesting therapy know that the therapy will not go on indeterminately. Short-term treatment has wide use in the field of therapy.[1] This is illustrated by the use of the techniques of behaviour modification and crisis intervention. Some writers suggest that even psychoanalysis, the classical long-term treatment method, has employed short-term treatment techniques as far back as Freud[2] The increased emphasis on short-term treatment in recent years seems largely due to the realization that therapy as a treatment method is a luxury for the few, and that the longer the length of treatment, the fewer the beneficiaries. The use of short-term treatment methods is partly aimed at trying to make effective therapeutic help available to a larger population.

The debate between advocates of long-term and short-term treatment methods has centered largely on the relative effectiveness of the methods. The advocates of long-term therapy suggest that short-term therapy is only effective with the mildest and most recent problems, while the advocates of short-term therapy claim that serious and long standing problems can be helped by their methods.[3] Malan, in his examination of the various studies that are used to support these different claims, suggests that the evidence they use is somewhat dubious, especially for those who claim that brief therapy is only effective with less serious problems.[4] His own research work leads him to the conclusion that "psychoanalytically based brief psychotherapy is possible."[5] If this conclusion is valid, and there is nothing in his research to suggest otherwise, then how much greater must be the potential for short-term models based on theories involving less time-consuming techniques than those based on psychoanalysis.

The use of short-term treatment techniques seems to depend as much, if not more, on the therapist as on the client's problem. Malan, in adding to a list of factors that might suggest longer treatment, adds four that relate to the analyst in the case of psychoanalysis. These are: a tendency towards passivity and the willingness to follow where the patient leads; the sense of timelessness conveyed to the patient; therapeutic perfectionism, and the increasing preoccupation with ever deeper and earlier experiences.[6] Insofar as therapy consists of an interaction between two or more people of which the therapist is one, judgements on indications and contra-indications about the use of any treatment method, including short and long-term models, must be, at least in part, influenced by the therapist.

Variables in the short-term model include the

number of interviews used per couple and the length of time during which the couple were actively engaged in marital therapy. Both of these variables are measurable. However, time and quantity are both relative concepts, as are the concepts of long and short.The use of time and number of sessions only in determining whether a therapeutic model is short or long is relative and also somewhat arbitrary. There is no agreement on the number of interviews or the length of time that determine short-term, even though Reid and Shyne suggest a limit of four interviews in a period not exceeding three months.[7]

The short-term treatment model is characterized by more than arbitrary cut-off points even though these are an integral part of the model. It consists of elements which transcend limitations of time and number and which affect the process of intervention itself. In his review of the briefer therapies, Small identifies three distinguishing features. These are the goals, the time factor and the methods used. However, he found no agreement among the authors about what is distinctly characteristic of the brief therapies. At most, the agreement would appear to be that the goals are more specific, the length of time shorter, and that the therapist uses more active methods than in the longer therapies, especially classical psychoanalysis.[8]

The short-term model used in Reinvestment Therapy is distinguished from those identified by Small by three different although somewhat similar features. The first of these is that the short-term model involves closed as opposed to open-ended treatment. This means that the therapist and couple both have a specified time within which to work. This does not necessarily mean that a rigid contract on time is entered into but that they know, at the very least, that the treatment is not indeterminate.

The second element in this short-term model is that the planning of termination constitutes an integral part of the therapy process. This arises out of the couple's knowledge that the therapist is working within limits of time and number of sessions. It differs from the long-term model where planning for termination arises only at the end and is usually seen as a specific aspect of the treatment that requires special handling.

The adoption of specific objectives immediately attainable is the third characteristic of the short-term model being used. This means that agreement between the therapist and the couple on the expectation of therapy is quite specific. There is no vague commitment to helping the couple with every or even most aspects of their marriage. Only goals that are attainable within a short period of time are agreed. Obviously the meaning of "attainable" is dependent on several factors, including the couple's abilities, the therapist's realistic estimation of his/her own abilities and the limits of the therapeutic methods employed.

These three factors are what characterize the short-term model used in Reinvestment Therapy. Their significance is derived from the use of the two measurable variables: number of interviews and length of time. The model is discussed under the headings of these two measurable variables. This discussion is against the backdrop of the overall study.

In discussing the number of sessions, it is necessary first to distinguish between individual sessions or interviews and joint sessions. When referring to the number of sessions or interviews offered in a contract, the reference is always to the number offered to each partner whether as a joint or individual session. Thus, for example, a contract of six sessions where the couple were seen jointly for four sessions and separately for two each, would amount to a total of eight sessions, but six sessions per partner as agreed by the contract.

Verbal contracts relating to the specific number of interviews being offered are always introduced in the first session. Although the number of interviews is specified, it is never arbitrary, and is always determined by the needs of the situation as seen at the time. Basically, the task to be achieved and the amount of therapy thought necessary for its performance are the factors of prime importance. The contract is flexible and usually, but not always, involves two stages.

The first stage consists of offering an initial contract in the region of four sessions. This number is used as it allows sufficient time for the couple to complete the engagement phase of the Reinvestment Therapy and to become involved in the exploration phase. The initial contract should allow for this transition, as it is only when a couple have progressed to the exploration phase that they can realistically evaluate the effectiveness of the Reinvestment Therapy.

An essential feature of this first stage in the contract is an agreement with the couple that the marital therapy be evaluated at the end of the stage. Explicit in the contract is an agreement by both the therapist and the couple to be honest in the evaluation, even if this means confronting the couple with their lack of motivation, or the therapist with his/her ineffectual efforts.

Another feature of this four-session contract is that it

excludes deciding on any long-term agreements. The therapy could conclude at the end of this stage if the couple felt that their relationship was sufficiently satisfactory to require no further help such as would be offered at the consolidation phase; or if there is lack of progress and it seems at the time that no progress is likely to occur. If on the other hand, the review shows a need to continue with the exploration phase or to move onto the consolidation phase, and there seems reasonable likelihood of it being beneficial, a further contract is offered. Sometimes a new beginning is necessary so a fresh contract around the engagement phase is offered. However, repeating contracts around this phase more than once is unlikely to be beneficial. It is with the offering of further contracts, other than a return to the engagement phase that the second stage begins.

The number of interviews in the second stage, as in the first stage, is determined by the situation. Usually it involves from two to four interviews. The major difference between the contract relating to the second stage and that of the first stage is that there is an expectation on the part of the therapist that therapy should terminate on completion of the newly-agreed contract. Even though further contracts could be agreed on completion of this stage, the therapeutic importance of anticipatory behaviour,[9] the result of the use of time-limited contracts, needs to be emphasized. The couple's expectation of improvement is considered central to the outcome. While they expect achievement of the objectives agreed in the contract, the couple also know that further agreement on help would be available if needed. A follow-up interview is often included as part of this contract or offered before termination.

The length of time during which the couple are actively engaged in Reinvestment Therapy is influenced by a number of factors other than the effectiveness of the therapy. Mainly, these consist of the nature of the therapy itself, the length of each therapy session, the frequency of interviews, and the points in time used for measuring the start and finish of therapy.

As explained already in this chapter, the nature of Reinvestment Therapy lends itself to the use of the short-term model, which includes the use of time limits. Other therapies—such as reflective, non-directive approaches—by their very nature tend to reject such time limits, with the length of time allowed being determined solely by the pace at which the therapy progresses. With Reinvestment Therapy time limits are used as a therapeutic tool, and are thus not just an end result but also a means to achieving the objectives of the therapy.

With regard to the length of each therapy session, the standard 50-minute hour is used as a model. However, this period can vary from a minimum of about 30 minutes to a maximum of 75 minutes approximately.

Weekly intervals are regarded as the desirable frequency for the initial sessions in the marital therapy. This frequency is seen as optimal for two reasons: it is long enough to allow sufficient time for the couple to work on the tasks emerging from the sessions, and short enough not to place too high an expectation on the couple to maintain change initially. In the later stages of the therapy the frequency can and usually is reduced progressively from every two weeks to three or possibly four, terminating with a follow-up some six weeks later. This frequency varies according to the couple. Any extension or shortening of the interval between sessions needs to be related to the learning of new behaviour.

As with the number of sessions, the frequency referred to here is the frequency with which any one partner is seen by the therapist. Thus a weekly frequency with each partner seen separately would be two sessions per week with each seen weekly, not one session with each fortnightly.

The start and finish of therapy is taken as the first and last session in which a couple either individually or jointly are seen. This means that the length of time is measured from the intake session through to the final follow-up interview which usually takes place about six weeks after the objective of the therapy has been achieved. Thus, the duration of therapy referred to here is the total duration of therapy using 50-minute sessions with a weekly frequency initially.

Although agreements on the length of time for marital therapy are included as a routine part of initial contract with couples, they tend to be more fluid than agreements on the number of sessions. To work with rigid time-schedules is not always possible or desirable. To do so requires control over variables that cannot easily be controlled. Success depends on the probability of three people being able to predict with accuracy their ability to meet at an agreed frequency within a specified time. Consequently, contracts about duration have of necessity to be flexible.

Though it does allow for the difficulties that may arise in agreeing on the precise total duration of the therapy, the contract does involve agreement on the expected length of each sesion and their frequency. Agreement on the number of sessions is meaningless if there is no agreement on these other elements. Four sessions with a monthly frequency is obviously quite different from four sessions with a weekly frequency.

Time as a variable is routinely discussed with each couple in the initial stages of the therapy. Usually this is a brief discussion and consists mainly of explanations. If a couple have difficulty agreeing to a set frequency for whatever reason, or are unable to keep to the frequency once it has been agreed, failing to keep appointments and thereby establishing a new frequency, the matter is given further discussion. The frequency is always planned and agreed to by the couple and the therapist. It is never left unplanned or allowed to develop simply on an *ad hoc* basis. Contracts can, of course, be reviewed or re-negotiated. Frequency of sessions is considered an important part of the therapy, and as such requires planning.

The measurable variables in the short-term model are those of number of interviews and duration of therapy. As indicated earlier, it is the combination of these two variables and the ways in which they are used that is of significance. Measuring the number of interviews without reference to the duration of therapy is largely meaningless, and vice versa.

The short-term model, then, has many important features. Most important for a therapeutic tool, it relies heavily on the couple's own expectations of therapy. These expectations in themselves can constitute a major determinant of the eventual outcome. Expectations of increased mutual satisfaction can therefore be a powerful motivating factor.

Another aspect of the couple's expectations, in addition to anticipation of outcome, is their expectations about the demands of Reinvestment Therapy. A couple who know what to expect are in a better position to make decisions than those who do not know. For example, knowing that a commitment to therapy will involve attending for a definite number of sessions on a weekly basis over a specified period of time makes it possible for the couple to plan. This planning could include such things as arranging babysitting and taking time off work. If a couple expect therapy to extend over an indefinite period of time, the uncertainties involved in making these arrangements could constitute a deterrent. In addition to this, the couple's expectations that at the end of Reinvestment Therapy the agreed objectives will have been achieved enables them to invest themselves in the efforts to achieve these changes even when they know that the end result is near at hand. This is analagous to the everyday occurrence of enduring temporary pain in order to achieve some long-term result. Short-term contracts, therefore, involve not just commitments on the part of the therapist to be available for an agreed number of sessions over a specified period of time, but also commitments on the part of the couple to attend. This is a part of the contract that can easily be overlooked even though it is an important aspect in the use of the short-term model as a therapeutic tool.

The short-term model consists essentially of the nature of the contract between the therapist and the couple. It is not simply the actual length of therapy, nor the use of arbitrary cut-off points. However, when limitations of time and number of sessions are introduced, the marital therapist and couple must come, both separately and jointly, to realistic expectations of each other.

NOTES

1. See W. Reid and H. Shyne, *Brief and Extended Casework* (New York 1967), E. Phillips, and D. Wiener, *Short-term Psychotherapy and Structural Behavior Change* (New York 1966); L. Bellak and L. Small, *Emergency Psychotherapy and Brief Psychotherapy* (New York 1965) and E. M. Goldberg, J. Gibbons and I. Sinclair, *Problems, Tasks and Outcomes: An Evaluation of Task-Centered Casework in Three Settings* (London 1985).

2. M. Balint, P. Ornstein and E. Balint, *Focal Psychotherapy* (London 1972), p. 7

3. D. Malan, *A Study of Brief Psychotherapy*(London 1963), p.v.

4. *Ibid*: p. 35.

5. *Ibid* p. 279.

6. *Ibid* pp. 8-9.

7. W. Reid and H. Shyne, *op. cit.*, p. 57.

8. W. Reid and H. Shyne, *op. cit.*, p. 57.

9. By the use of the term "anticipatory behaviour" is meant the inclusion of an individual's expectation as a determinant of future behaviours as a kind of self-fulfiling prophecy. In this case it refers to the expectation on the part of the couple that certain objectives are obtainable and will be achieved within a specified time.

Chapter 10

The Challenge of Reinvestment Therapy

The main theme running throughout this book is that society is changing and that marriage is changing with it. Changes in society are affecting marriage both as a social institution and as a personal relationship. As regards the social institution of marriage, the changes are reflected in the increased expectation of having individual needs for intimacy met within marriage. It is this changed expectation which presents a major challenge not only to individuals in marriage but also to marital therapists and to society in general.

The challenge to all three groups (i.e. couples, marital therapists, and society) centres on one primary issue: the expansion and development of sources of affection in marriage. It is not sufficient to assume that love exists in a relationship simply because a couple are in the roles of husband and wife. This love needs to be manifested in their actions and attitudes towards one another. People's expectations of having this basic human need met are increasingly becoming the cornerstone upon which the future of the relationship depends.

First, let us look at what the challenge means for couples. In order to develop sources of affection in a relationship, a couple must come to a realization that they control what happens between them. (This may not be true for couples who experience many stress factors such as severe emotional and material deprivation.) Many couples coming for marital therapy do not seem to appreciate the fact that they control their own relationship. They tend to look towards external causes or controls. The last place they look is to themselves. They blame each other, their families of origin, their work, their friends or even destiny. This does not mean that they are unaffected by their environment. Of course they are. It is their handling of this that is of crucial importance. These couples have lost control of their relationship. Thus, they cannot do anything effectively about expanding and developing sources of affection in each other until they gain or regain control.

Lucy and Noel illustrate this point well. Both were very keen to resolve their difficulties. Both agreed that they had fallen into a "rut." Noel felt that his marriage was much affected by his work. He was a sales representative paid on a commission basis. When sales were poor he was in a generally poor mood and tended to be irritable and withdrawn at home. When sales were good there was less conflict at home. Lucy agreed with these observations, saying that Noel's father behaved much the same way. While she disliked his behaviour she had no expectation that it would ever be any different.

Apart from any other difficulties between this couple, they were trapped by their resignation to a belief that their marriage interaction was affected by factors beyond their control, i.e. destiny and Noel's work.

In this frame of mind they were unable to look to themselves for change. Lucy accepted that Noel, by virtue of being a member of his own family would be "moody," and Noel blamed his work. It was not until Noel accepted that he controlled his part in the interaction with Lucy, and until Lucy accepted that Noel was not locked into patterns of behaviour by destiny, that they could begin to look for new ways of responding to each other. With this acceptance, they were able to find new and more rewarding patterns that led to an increased exchange of affection between them. Thus, the challenge of reinvestment for Noel and Lucy was to reclaim control of their own relationship.

Another challenge facing couples, expecially those who are having relationship difficulties, is to be able to see where problems are simply symptoms of a more basic, but manageable, underlying cause. In the context of the arguments presented in this book, expecially in Chapter Three, many of these problems can be seen as likely to be manifestations of changed expectations of marriage resulting from the influences of changes in society. The underlying factor is often role incompatability, as discussed in Chapter Four, with the partners failing to meet each other's needs for affection.

Take, for example, the relationship between Lily and Harry. Lily showed symptoms of depression and was receiving treatment for it from her G.P. Harry felt that once her depression was "cured" all would be well in their marriage. He was very tolerant of Lily's depression, and made many adjustments in his life to accommodate it, such as taking time off work to bring her for treatment. Lily, however, showed little sign of improving and was feeling more and more inadequate. Her self-esteem was almost completely eroded and she felt confused and frustrated because of the depression. She thought of her husband as a good partner, but felt guilty because she did not feel close to him and even wondered if she loved him any more.

This unhappy state continued until Lily came to realize that while Harry provided for most of her others needs, he also seemed to keep her in a dependent and powerless state in which her needs for closeness were not being met. This realisation, coupled with an acknowledgement that her expectations of closeness were reasonable, had the effect of releasing her from much of her feeling of guilt, depression and self-doubt. At first she reacted with anger. But, as Harry began reaching out emotionally and also began to be open himself in expressing his own needs for closeness, they responded positively to each other. As they both continued to express intimacy and respond to one another with emotional understanding, Lily's position of dependency gradually began to change. Having gone beyond the surface problems, the couple were able to expand and develop sources of affection in each other that until now had been screened by the "depression."

Rory and Ann experienced a somewhat similar situation. Ann stayed at home after the birth of their first child and worked hard at being a good "housekeeper." The house was always immaculate, as were her children. She was a good cook, took care of her own appearance, was efficient and in general performed the role of housewife admirably. Rory, however, did not seem to appreciate her excellence and needless to say Ann was not too happy with his lack of appreciation. The more unhappy she was, the more she strove for perfection, and the more she tried the more unappreciative and dissatisfied Rory became. Then he protested that the house had become more important than he was, and insisted that what he really wanted was someone to relax with, to be tender towards, and to share with. He wanted, as he put it, "a lover, not a housekeeper."

It was difficult for Ann to come to terms with this information. Her love for Rory was expressed by cooking him special meals, bringing him breakfast in bed, or buying him a new shirt. Being alone with Rory, sharing her thoughts, her feelings, her fears, her joys and her aspirations, was new to her. Being tender, and for Ann this meant being vulnerable, was a risk she found difficult to take. However, she did succeed in expressing her love for Rory. Eventually they were both able to see their different ways of expressing affection. By releasing themselves and one another from fixed perceptions of marital roles, they successfully provided scope for an expansion of affection in their relationship.

Many problems in marriage have their origin in rigid role definitions. This is particularly so with sex-role stereotyping whereby husband and wives find themselves locked into narrowly defined roles based on sex. There is an increasing amount of evidence to show the negative effects of this type of role restriction.[1] Reinvestment Therapy offers a way out of this trap for both partners by helping them to challenge these socially defined roles. Thus, for many couples, Reinvestment Therapy is a re-negotiation of marital roles. Through this re-negotiation of roles the couple are enable to find new sources of affection.

Some couples are unable to expand the sources of affection in their marriage because they tend to focus attention on some personality factor in their partner. These projections tend to get fixed on such causes as emotional immaturity, inability to be intimate, excessive dependency, over-controlling behaviour, rigid personality and an almost endless list of similar causes located in the partner.

This process is less threatening to the "self" if blame for the problems encountered in the relationship are projected onto someone else. However, such projections prevent the resolution of the problems, as illustrated by the examples of both the case of Noel and Lucy and that of Harry and Lily.

For as long as problems in the relationship are attributed to some personality factor of one's partner, it releases the other from responsibility for the relationship, and also allows that person to avoid having any expectations of change. This position not only prevents the resolution of problems in the relationship, but actually contributes to maintaining them. The challenge of reinvestment for these couples is first to come to a realization and acceptance that neither of them are necessarily to blame. Only then can they look to elements such as role compatibility and expression of affection in their relationship for a solution. Unhappiness in a relationship is a major stress, and as such it is likely to produce some behaviour that can be labelled problematic. Focusing attention on this kind of behaviour instead of on the emotional distance which has brought it about is unlikely to produce happiness in the relationship.

Another way in which couples can get locked into sterile interaction is by continuing to focus on those aspects of each other that they found intially attractive, such as the woman's trim figure and the man's success with a local football team, both of which attributes may have long since gone. With the passage of time, neither person is the same as when they first met. Apart from being older, they will have changed in many other respects. Most likely they will have become parents, have increased responsibilities, have changed physically and have altered many of their life roles. In addition they will have been affected by changes in society, their environment, the media, social movements, a hightened awareness of their own place in society and other factors originating outside themselves.

Affection grows and develops in relationships which grow and develop as the individuals themselves grow and develop. The affection is found in a couple's ability to understand one another and to generate in each other a feeling of uniqueness. For some couples who never moved beyond their initial attraction for each other, the bond becomes based on simply being accustomed to one another. The relationship has little excitement. Regrets are expressed for the loss of the "spark" that was theirs originally and each wonders how the relationship which has now become so dull could have once been so good.

The challenge of reinvestment for couples centres around finding new ways of releasing affection. When old ways, such as those which are vested in the institutional role of spouse, are no longer sufficient, there is little use in simply expecting or demanding affection. This tends to happen when couples see their relationship as being controlled by factors outside themselves, or when they focus on the performance of traditional marriage roles or project blame for marital unhappiness onto some personality factor in their spouse, or when the couple continue to base their relationship on those aspects of each other that brought them together initially.

New sources of affection can be explored in any relationship. For many couples these are found in the uniqueness of each of the two individuals in the relationship. It is this personal, intimate self when released in a tender caring relationship, which provides the springboard for an expansion of the source of affection for these couples. This is what constitutes the differences between marriage, an institutional relationship, and marriage, a personal relationship. The challenge lies in achieving this.

For the marital therapist the challenges are similar to those facing the couple. They consist of helping the couple to find new sources of affection in each other. Much of this has been discussed in Chapters Five to Eight. There are, however, two aspects which have particular relevance here.

The first of these has to do with the therapist's definition of the couple's problem. This means that the therapist needs to be open to several possible causes for the unhappiness in the relationship, including the impact of social change. All couples seeking Reinvestment Therapy are likely to have sexual

difficulties and poor communication, be emotionally
upset and be unable to manage conflict effectively,
irrespective of the underlying cause of their problems.
Obviously, if these are merely symptoms of some
other cause, there is little value in trying to change
them without reference to what is underpinning them
in the first place.

It is at this point that the marital therapist is faced
with a challenge. As seen in Chapter One, there is a
tendency to attribute marital problems to a single
cause, i.e. the personalities of the individuals who are
married. The challenge is to see people who have
marital problems as being no different, in many cases,
from the rest of the population. That is, the challenge is
to see them as mature, healthy and emotionally stable
individuals. It is true that some are not, but this is quite
different from saying that all are not. Finding
alternative explanations is a further challenge. In this
book one such alternative put forward is that people in
their marriages are affected by change in society which
brings about changes in their expectations. These
expectations are related to the need for intimacy and a
desire to have one's needs for affection met in
marriage. When this does not occur, unhappiness is
likely to result, irrespective of how it is expressed.

The second major area of concern for the
reinvestment therapist is that of translating this focus
into a therapeutic programme. For many couples the
programme will most likely take the form of coaching
on how to show empathy, caring and understanding.
For some this will require taking a risk, as they
probably have protected themselves against hurt by
being emotionally distant. The coaching can be done in

a variety of ways. For example, it can involve instructing the couple on how to relate in a particular manner, or it can be done by modelling the behaviour for them in the therapy sessions. This coaching is done in the context of helping the couple to expand their understanding of and interest in each other.

Since the focus of Reinvestment Therapy as advocated in this book is on the mutual meeting of affectional needs, it is important to look at the role played by the sex of the marital therapist. Expectations of fulfilment in a relationship are of necessity based on concepts of equality. Liberation in marriage, either for men or for women cannot be attained if either of them are stuck in stereotyped sex roles. This also applies to the liberation of the therapist. The therapist by simply being present is not neutral. The sex of the therapist needs to be kept in mind. While marital therapists may wish to be neutral, their sex does not make this possible. Marriage is a relationship between a male and a female, and when a third party is introduced, it tips the balance either towards one sex or the other. The challenge is not to be sexually neutral, but to be sexually fair by being aware of the influence of one's own sex in the therapy process. The insight that everything is perceived in the mode of the receiver, or that you don't see things as they are, but as you are, is just as true for the therapist as it is for the individuals who are involved in the therapy process.

Reinvestment Therapy, therefore, challenges the marital therapist's definitions of marital disharmony and the role played in the therapy by the therapist's sex. Both of these challenges are crucial for any marital therapist. Reinvestment Therapy, however, takes these challenges a step further by providing an approach to marital therapy that takes account of the sex bias of the therapist and the theories that underpin the marital therapy. A charge increasingly being made against many approaches to therapy is that they are based on male-orientated theories that contribute to keeping women in "sick"and dependent roles. Such a charge (and there is a volume of evidence to support the charge) has far-reaching implications when levelled at marital therapy. Reinvestment Therapy makes no assumptions about roles in marriage other than that they are multiple and can be shared between partners in whatever way meets their needs. Likewise, it makes no assumptions about attributes appropriate to either sex. Couples are seen as individuals within a systen which is itself constantly in a process of change as it interacts with the social environment of which it is a part.

Finally, let us look at some of the challenges reinvestment poses for society. Probably the most fundamental challenge is to address the question of priorities. Can a society plan for the sort of family it sees as ideal, while simultaneously pursuing economic goals that may well be in conflict with these ideals?

Take, for example, a developing economy like that of Ireland. Over the past few decades successive governments have followed programmes of industrialization. These programmes have involved the adoption of certain industrial values such as individualism and competition that could well be seen to be in conflict with family values like collectivism and co-operation. Then does the economic need, such as the efficient running of a plant, take precedence over family occasions like births, weddings and deaths? It would appear that the family, in theory considered the primary social unit, is in fact becoming relegated to the position of serving the needs of our economic institutions.

It has been argued throughout this book that social change brings about change in marriage and the family. No society can realistically expect the family as a social institution to remain static, while it vigorously changes other major social institutions. There is little use in bemoaning the loss of the "traditional" family if the "traditional" society which maintained it no longer exists. If our commitment to marriage and the family is as strong as our exhortations to preserve some long-since vanished ideal, should we not as a society take more active measures to promote the type of family we wish to have, and develop our other institutions around that plan? In this way our economic institutions, for example, might become the servant of the family, instead of vice versa.

Marriage is both a private and a public affair. How individual couples live out their relationships is private to them. How couples in general do so is a public matter. Depression, alcoholism, physical violence and other manifestations of unmet needs in marriage are as much a public concern as they are private. So, too, are divorce and re-marriage. It is not possible to separate marriage from the society of which it is a part or to separate society from marriage. Each influences the other. Blaming individuals for their marital stress is as futile as blaming couples for changing the institution of marriage. The marital therapist who retreats into a search for personal causes for marital unhappiness is in effect doing just this. So too is the policy-maker who fails to take account of the forces of social change when divising family policy.

Marriage is going through a process of change just like society. The effect of these changes is that marriage is becoming a highly specialised social system based on bonds of love and affection. In it men and women have a great potential for personal fulfilment and affirm. By seeing this potential and embarking on its realization, we as individuals in marriage and as members of society in general have an exciting and rewarding challenge ahead.

NOTES

1. M. Cullen and T. Morrissey, *Women and Health* (Dublin 1985)

Bibliography

Anderson, H. and H. A. Goolishan, "Human Systems as Linguistic Systems: Preliminary and Evolving Ideas about the Implications for Clinical Theory," *Family Process* 27, 1988 pp.371-393.

Bahr S., "Marital Dissolution Laws," *Journal of Family Issues* September 1983, pp.455-66.

Balint M., P. Ornstein and E. Balint, *Focal Psychotherapy* (London 1972)

Bannister K. and L. Pinus, *Shared Phantasy in Marital Problems: Therapy in a Four-Person Relationship* (London 1976)

Barker P., *Basic Family Therapy* (London 1981)

Bellak L. and L. Small, *Emergency Psychotherapy and Brief Psychotherapy* (New York 1965)

Bennis W., K. Benne and R. Chin, eds., *The Planning of Change* (New York 1961)

Bernard J., *The Future of Marriage* (Harmondsworth 1976)

Buckley W., *Sociology and Modern Systems Theory* (New Jersey 1967)

Buckley W., *Modern Systems Reseach for the Behavioural Scientist* (Chicago 1968)

Burgess E., H. Locke and M. Thomes, *The Family: From Institution to Companionship* 4th ed. (New York 1971)

Carter, B. and M. McGoldrick, *The Changing Family Life Cycle* (New York 1988)

Coser R., *The Family: Its Structure and Functions* (New York 1964)

Cullen M. and T. Morrissey, *Women and Health* (Dublin 1988)

Dominian J., *Marital Breakdown* (Harmondsworth 1968)

Dreitzel H. ed., *Family, Marriage, and the Struggle of the Sexes* (New York 1972)

Dryden W., ed., *Marital Therapy in Britain* (London 1985)

Family Studies Unit, *The Changing Family* (Dublin 1984)

Ferri E., *Growing Up in a One-Parent Family* (London 1976)

Fromm, E. *The Art of Loving* (London 1975)

Germain, C.B. and A. Gitterman, *The Life Model of Social Work Practice* (New York 1980)

Goldberg E. M., J. Gibbons and L. Sinclair, *Problems, Tasks and Outcomes: An Evaluation of Task-Centered Casework in Three Settings* (London 1988)

Goldstein H., *Social Work Practice: A Unitary Approach* (Columbia 1973)

Goode W., *The Family* (New Jersey 1964)

Gorer G., *Sex and Marriage in England Today* (St Albans Herts. 1973)

Hannon D. and L. Katsiaouni, *Traditional Families: From Culturally Prescribed to Negotiated Roles in Farm Families* (Dublin 1977)

Harris, C.C., *The Family and Industrial Society* (London 1983)

Hearn G., ed., *The General Systems Approach* (New York 1969)

Heus M. and A. Pincus, *The Creative Generalist: A Guide to Social Work Practice* (Barneveld Wisconsin 1986)

Hunt M., *Sexual Behavior in the 1970s* (New York 1974)

Janchill M., "Systems Concepts in Casework Theory and Practice," *Social Casework* 50, 2, (1969), pp. 74-82.

Keniston K. and The Carnegie Council on Children, *All Our Children* (New York 1978)

Kiely G., "Social Change and Marital Problems," *British Journal of Guidance and Counselling*, January 1984, pp.80-89.

Komarovsky M., *Blue Collar Marriage* (New York 1962)

Laing R.D., *The Divided Self* (Harmondsworth 1960)

Lamanna M. and A. Riedman, *Marriage and Families*, 2nd ed. (Belmont 1983)

Landis J. and M. Landis, *Building a Successful Marriage*, 5th ed. (New Jersey 1968)

Lippit R., J. Watson and B. Westley, *Dynamics of Planned Change* (New York 1958)

Malan D., *A Study of Brief Psychotherapy* (London 1963)

Maturana H.R. and F.J. Varela, *The Tree of Knowledge: The Biological Roots of Human Understanding* (Boston 1987)

Melville K., *Marriage and Family Today* (New York 1977)

Minuchin S., *Family Therapy Technique* (Cambridge 1981)

Monane J., *A Sociology of Human Systems* (New York 1967).

Ogburn W. and N. Nimkoff, *A Handbook of Sociology*, 5th ed. (London 1964)

Parsons T. and R. Bales, *Family, Socialization and the Interaction Process* (London 1956)

Parsons T., *Societies: Evolutionary and Comparative Perspectives* (New Jersey 1966)

Phillips E. and D. Weiner, *Short-term Psychotherapy and Structural Behaviour Change* (New York 1966)

Pincus A. and A. Minahan, *Social Work Practice: Model and Method* (Illinois 1973)

Reid W. and H. Shyne, *Brief and Extended Casework* (New York 1967)

Reiss I.,"Towards a Sociology of the Heterosexual Love Relationship," *Marriage and Family Living* (May 1960), pp.139-45.

Reiss I., *The Family Systems in America* (New York 1971)

Schofield M., *The Sexual Behaviour of Young People* (London 1965)

Shorter E., *The Making of the Modern Family* (London 1976)

Skolnick A., *The Intimate Environment* (Boston 1973)

Skynner A., *One Flesh: Separate Persons* (London 1976)

Specht H. and A. Vickery, *Integrating Social Work Methods* (London 1977)

Sussman M. and S. Steinmetz eds., *Handbook of Marriage and the Family* (New York 1987)

Toner J., *The Experience of Love* (Washington 1968)

Winch R., *The Modern Family* , rev. ed. (New York 1963)

DATE DUE